My Soul Looks Back

Life After Incarceration

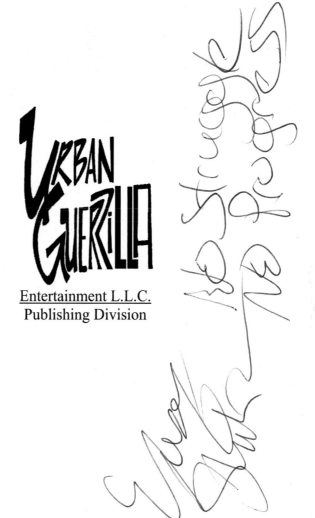

Entertainment L.L.C.
Publishing Division

51499>

Printed in the United States of America

1st Printing: Feb 15, 2012

ISBN: 978-1-937183-24-0

Library of Congress Control Number: 200892359

www.yusefshakur.org

Dedications

To my sons DeAngelo & Kobie

ACKNOWLEDGEMENTS

To everybody that has supported me locally, nationally and internationally thank you from the bottom of my heart because your support has made all the difference in the world....

To all the doubters thank you for the inspiration!!!!!!

Praise for
"My Soul Looks Back: Life After Incarceration"

"Ultimately, this book is a tool. For all of us who've ever struggled to love and live with the millions of men and women who are victims of mass incarceration."
-dream hampton

"This is a perfect story of redemption, perfect story of atonement and the perfect story of a man... Yusef pushes me to be a better police chief."
-Chief of Police, Ralph Godbee

"Yusef Shakur has done it again. By allowing us into his world he has shown all a blueprint for all to take the much needed journey from victim to victor. This is a must read."
-Ryan Mack, CNN Contributor & Author of Living in the Village

"Yusef Shakur is proof that where you start in life doesn't dictate how you finish… Yusef Shakur has gone from convict to community leader. His goal to motivate and inspire young people in the City of Detroit is an amazing story."
-Huel Perkins, Detroit Fox 2 News

"When I've seen him do a one-on-one with young Black men that he's trying to keep from making mistakes he's made… It's powerful."
-City Councilman, Ken Cockrel, Jr.

"From your personal experience you have given hope to individuals who may otherwise feel their situation is hopeless."
- John Conyers, Congressman

"Yusef Shakur's tireless energy and tenacity in working with youth, especially the disenfranchised is unprecedented."
-Hansen Clarke, Congressman

"Some may call it a blessing, others may say it's a second chance, whatever Yusef's turnaround is called, it's nothing short of inspiring. Yusef is living proof that a life that begins on the wrong tracks, can indeed be saved."
-State Senator, Bert Johnson

"Yusef Shakur has a message that needs to be heard; that is giving a 2nd chance to those who redeem themselves in prison."
-Michigan Chronicle Senior Editor, Bankole Thompson
"Yusef's freedom did not occur when he was released from incarceration, it happened when he reclaimed his soul, which for years was being held hostage by fear, pain and anger. The story of his poor decision making as a youth and the consequences that follow plays out in under-served communities all across the country, yet he provides a blueprint for how to re-invent one's self and how not to be defined by low expectations."
-James Tate, City Councilman

Yusef B. Shakur is truly an inspiration to all of us who work for equality and justice. His deep dedication to progressive social change, which he started in his own neighborhood, is spilling over to many other places like a tidal wave through his wonderful work, monumental speeches, and brilliant writings. Yusef is a champion of peace and prosperity for all!
- David A. Kinney, Ph.D., Professor of Sociology, Central Michigan University

Shakur takes us on a journey.... As he brilliantly weaves together historical, economic and socio-political analysis with personal examples of how these things work on a day to day level in his own struggle for survival.
-Dr. Karen M. Gagne, Assistant Professor of Sociology, University of Wisconsin-Pkatteville

Contents

Foreword:

When I'm at community meetings in Detroit, no matter how small, big or fringe, Yusef "Bunchy" Shakur is the constant. He changes the room he enters but he's never interested in a takeover; he often listens long before he participates or speaks. His contributions are often thoughtful, even when he has to steer the action in a completely different direction. That direction is often home, to the actual neighborhoods----as opposed to an activated and invigorated downtown. In Detroit's neighborhoods are boys and girls and men and women trapped in the cycles of mass incarceration. No one in our city's neighborhoods is free from the affects of prison. We all "have" someone going in or coming out of a prison plantation, the only place in this country where slavery is still legal. In "My Soul Looks Back" Yusef asks us to journey past the visiting room (even as he scolds us for largely abandoning our loved ones behind the walls, rarely writing, barely visiting).

We are, by now, all familiar with the facts and stats of mass incarceration. We know the United States counts more than 2 million prisoners, another 5 million are tethered to prison through probation or some other court supervision, their freedoms handicapped by sandy and arbitrary rules that often return them to jail or prison. We know prisons are a growing industry, that increasingly prisons are privatized, providing near free labor for the biggest corporations in the country. We know that inside, Black and Brown men and women are represented disproportionately, and that our families are separated and suffer because of mass incarceration more than Whites. We know that the war on drugs is and was only ever a war on the poor. We know that while Whites are more likely to use drugs, we are more likely to have the medical problem of addiction treated with incarceration. We know our boys are stalked, harassed and murdered by police as prepubescent's and rarely make it to 25 without having some interface with what can only morbidly be called "the law".

But with "My Soul Looks Back" Yusef "Bunchy" Shakur takes us behind and beyond those walls, inside the psychological spaces of prisons, where the captors and the enslaved form alternate, hidden societies with their own codes and pathologies. "In prison it is rare to hold a healthy conversation," he writes. "Prisoners and prison guards often talk with the intent to try and get over on one another. Most conversations are centered on exploitive relationships." He explains how near impossible healthy post-prison interactions are after decades of "animalistic behavior" where men and women survive only because they are good at exploiting one another. He unpacks the cycles of abuse--all kinds of abuse---and how these prisoners bring these amplified pathologies home to lovers, children and neighbors. The profound sense of isolation prison creates for the imprisoned, long after they're no longer physically behind bars. But even then Shakur is as capable of imagining new ways of being too:

"One of the biggest challenges I faced after leaving prison was feeling like I had no one I could turn to. In prison I was always able to develop a codependent type of relationship with at least one of the hundreds of prisoners I was encaged with. I could go to that person and borrow a stamp, toothpaste, soap, noodles, etc and they could do the same with me. I was also able to bare my soul with a person who wouldn't judge me and vice versa. That type of relationship is so important in human development. I know many us have conditioned our minds to believe that we are an Island to ourselves but that is a *lie* that we have made ourselves believe! We are all codependent of each other in some form or fashion. It is just a matter of developing strong relationships with dependable people that we can rely on in our time of need. We should ask ourselves; out of the hundreds of people we know how many of them can we count on? That is an important question we should be asking ourselves everyday in our quest to be the best human beings we can be."

That is ultimately Yusef "Bunchy" Shakur's greatest strength; his ability to imagine a world beyond this broken one. Many in Detroit know his story; it is Toni Morrison style epic; he met his father for the first time when they were imprisoned together. A former gang banger he works in Detroit's roughest neighborhoods, his own, to restore honor and code, to reconcile street warriors and to, as he often says, "restore the neighbor back in the hood." Yusef knows this thinking and these slogans can be real solutions but only if we first look honestly and deeply and longly at mass incarceration's psychic toll. Here he does both, remembering his near past as a prisoner. He takes responsibility for the behavior that got him there, even as he describes the conditions that made his path seem the only one. His retelling of the story of his romantic love affair with his life partner is sometimes painful, often triumphant and always a road map. Ultimately, this book is a tool. For all of us who've ever struggled to love and live with the millions of men and women who are victims of mass incarceration.

dream hampton

Introduction

Good afternoon,

I have to say of all the things I have been asked to do since I have been in law enforcement for the last 24 years, Yusef I want you to know that this is the greatest honor I have had to speak. Today as we celebrate your life, as we celebrate what you have accomplished, as we celebrate the fact that I have a new little brother that I totally love, we are joined at the hip and as long as God allows me breath I am not ashamed of being a friend of Yusef. That is my man's, so let's give Yusef a huge hand. You all probably think that it is strange, especially when you saw flyers going around about a former Zone 8 and the Chief of Police as the keynote speaker as he celebrates his life, but to me this is the perfect story of redemption, perfect story of atonement and the perfect story of a man; a grown man who on life's journey and God's path brought him. He went through a period of discovering himself. People incarcerated his body, but God allowed his mind to become free during that period of incarceration as he met his father, as he ultimately became an author and advocate for his community post incarceration. As he speaks out and he talks about issues that other people are afraid to talk about, as he talks about them in terms that are not politically correct and will tickle our fancy and make us really start think about things in a more dynamic way. Yusef you pushed me to be a better police chief and I appreciate you for that!

There has to be a different conversation in this community. There has to be a much different conversation in America about what we have done to our young African America men, what we have done to our communities and how incarceration and the disproportionate number of Black and Brown people that have been incarcerated has done to our communities. If locking up Black people was the answer to the crime problem we would have been out of it a long time ago, so it is obvious that is not the answer. So, you may think it is strange that a police chief is talking in these types of terms, but my end game for the police department in the City of Detroit is for Detroit to be a safe city and locking people up and incarcerating them and then creating an environment where it is destined for them to fail is not a system that I want to partake in. But we have to change the conversation about how this system works. There are four cornerstones of what we need to do as a society and specifically in Detroit, which is 85% African American. We are the Black Mecca! People should look at us from all across the country to figure out what we are doing here. What is it about Detroit? What is so special about Detroit that we get it right when everybody else can't? I think we are making our way that way because of the relationship between the police and the community. In my opinion we are starting to make some strides towards doing it the right way. The reason that way it is easy for me to do is because I was born and raised in the City of Detroit. I love this city. I am a native of the Eastside of Detroit. A couple of times I used some pretty big words because I have a Masters Degree and I am still paying my student loan, so as long I am paying for these words I'ma use them. But don't get it twisted, I will go there and I say "ain't" and all that stuff. So, don't think I am un-educated when I do that, but I am just real about who I am and what God has done for me. We all are stories of redemption, if we are honest. The bible says "We have all sinned and come short of the glory of God." Some of us just haven't got caught. Now if we are real about where we are at in our lives and our maturation of where we are going and how God is developing us, all of us have a Yusef story, but all of us don't have the courage to tell the world what we have done wrong and expose ourselves in such a way that Yusef has where he is not ashamed of where God has brought him from and where God is taking him to. Now I don't want you to get twisted or concerned of which God I am talking about. Rather you serve Allah or rather you served my lord and savior Jesus Christ, let's not get twisted about that. If you want to get to downtown Detroit, I live on the Eastside and the way I get downtown, I take I-94 westbound and then I take I-75 south, and if you live on the Westside you have to take I-94 eastbound and then take I-75 south. No matter what path we take to get downtown, if that is our destination I can't get mad at you about the path you choose to take. So, we need to stop all this arguing and fighting about rather it is Allah or rather it is Jesus Christ and we all need to understand that there is a path that we all are taking to get to a destination. Now the destination that we all are trying to get to I hope, I think we all are talking about is a safe Detroit. A Detroit where our women can walk and not be molested, where we can go to stores and not worry about thugs taking over our corners. That is the kind of Detroit that we are talking about. But we have to be real about who we are and what we are going to fight, and as long as we keep fighting each other about stupid stuff, which I think it's real stupid to fight about who is the most moral. That is really a bad conversation to have. So, I love my brother Yusef because Yusef has an uncanny ability to bring together politicians, police chiefs, rich folks, poor folks and folks from all walks of life and make us have a conversation that is completely different than the conversation that we been having, because we been caught up in this who is the biggest Negro syndrome. Let's be real about it; about who can conquer the biggest corner and talk about the biggest program that I run and pat yourself on the back because I am the savior of Detroit. Unless we all get ourselves together and get a long and figure out how to work together and roll up our sleeves like Yusef and go out where the people are and talk to the real people, we not going to change the problem anyway. So, Yusef I thank you for enlightening us and enlightening your community. Leadership is not position, it is action. So, many of us get caught up on what our titles are, that is why I love Councilmen Tate and Spivey. These are two real men who are not caught up in titles and they look at the end game of pulling people together to work for the betterment of the community to make sure we have access to the things that we need to do things the right way.

So, to stand here and talk about Yusef for me is real easy and you would think that we have known each other for 20, 30 or 40 years, and that really is not the case. I met Yusef when we started having a meeting with Dr. Rev. Wendell Anthony when violence really started to take a different tone. It was right on the heels of the killing of Ayanna Jones. It was a real tenuous situation in this city, because we were at a point where people were talking about how we utilized the gang squad and how the police department was relating with young people, and I really believe we were at a tipping-point. Yusef came in the conversation and you have all these people with these titles and heavy weight doctorate degrees, PhD's and masters degrees and talking about white papers and research and what the demographics says and Yusef just began to talk in real terms about what the streets was saying, and really broke it down to us that if we really don't change the way we address our young people and we look at some concepts and look at how we deal with folks and how we deal with our community, this thing is really going to blow up. I really started to look at that young man and we had a very brief interaction and everybody was getting all upset saying Yusef you have to calm down and you need to be more politically correct because you gone offend somebody. But you know damnit, it is time that we start offending somebody, because if you continue to do the same thing that you been doing and you expect a different result then that is a definition of insanity, and something ought to make you mad! Now the bible says "be angry, but sin not." There ought to be a righteous indignation when our young people can't walk the street without being shot down by an AK-47. There ought to be a righteous indignation when our young ladies can't walk from school to home and home to school without worrying about being molested by old perverts like us. So, there ought to be somebody mad enough to raise some hell in this community, to get us activated and get us on fire to do the right thing!

So, Yusef I thank you!
Don't lose that fire!
Don't let anybody take that edge from you!
Be Yusef!
Do you brother!
I love you for being you!
Don't let anybody make you politically correct!
Don't let anybody change your activism!
Don't change you!
Love your people and be proud of who you are, because I am going to love you anyhow!

The principle tenants of Christianity, if we really gone talk and have some real talk… Can we have some real talk? It is about unconditional love. Jesus don't love you because of, He loves you in spite of and if we are going to be a real community that makes real change and really engage each other in real conversations, first of all, we have to be real about who we are. We all have sinned and come short of the glory of God, but the point is once you make a mistake as my dad has always taught me, that a mistake is not a mistake, if you learn something from it. Then after you learn something from it what do you do to engage somebody else to make sure that they don't go down the same path that you did? My father is 5 foot 5 and is one of the greatest and strongest men I have ever met in my life, but my dad told me that you ain't nothing but 5 foot 5 either boy, but if you stand on my shoulders we 10 feet tall and you can see a lot farther if you stand on my shoulders. So, we have a responsibility to our community. We need to stop labeling people that come back as returning citizens. You are not a felon. Don't let anybody define who you are or give you a title. You are a child of God. You are fearfully and wonderfully made by the hand of God and when God made you He said you were good and very good. He didn't say you were a felon. He didn't say you were an ex nothing. So, don't let anybody box you in and tell you who you are. You are who God said you are. So, Yusef that is why I love you man and appreciate you, because you have not allowed your circumstances to define you. We have to start empowering ourselves and learn who we are. Yusef, correct me if I am wrong, but it was during that period of incarceration when you had a chance to meet your father, where you learned who you were and you learned your values and what you had to give back that you made a decision as a man that you weren't going back there. That is why you are one of the most powerful fathers I know, because you are a father to your children and you love your community. That is what we have to do, have a period of enlightenment. Life is not about what happened to you, but it is how you respond. How are we going to respond Detroit? That is the question. Yusef Shakur, my brother today is a day of celebration and we want to give you your flowers while you live, because you earned them and deserve them brother. Yusef engaged me and said bro I want to be involved and I want to change this community. If we had more people who had the guts to roll up their sleeves and do what Yusef does, say what he says, go where he goes and not just drive by the problem and pretend like it is going to fix itself, then Detroit would be a much better place. So, Yusef on this day I honor you, I love you brother as we are joined in the struggle to resurrect a city we both love, Detroit! You are leading the charge and we all need to follow your example of atonement, transformation and redemption and Detroit will make a comeback sooner than later.

Chief of Police
Ralph Godbee
February 26, 2011

xvi

Coming Home

Chapter 1

There were no words that could explain the elation that I felt after earning parole. It had been a long time coming and a well deserved victory after having received four flops (parole denials) by the parole board. Although I had no major assault or fighting infractions in six years, I had been deemed a "menace to society" so they had no intention of releasing me from prison without a fight. The fact that I had earned my GED, participated in numerous prison programs and was even the fact that I had three strikes against me; one being that I was *young*, two I was *Black* and three, I was a *militant*! Before they released me they were hell bent on breaking me by any means necessary. However, what they failed to realize was that although I had entered prison as a *broken man*, I refused to leave that way. Nothing that they could have done to me behind those walls would have defeated my spirit, because I had fully embraced my new desire to be a souljah for my people and I was prepared to accept my fate, whatever that was. I overstood what came with the territory of being a *revolutionary*.

Because of the lack of support many prisoners receive from the community and their families, the prison administration and the parole board are able to *wreak havoc* on them. Many prisoners have been left for dead within the belly of the beast and are mentally, spiritually and physically tortured by their captors. There is an innumerable amount of prisoners who have not received a letter, phone call or visit from their family members in decades. Some have never received any communication at all.

Unfortunately the communities, including the family members that they've left behind have bought into the negative hype that is perpetuated by the mass media about prisoners and the prison system. So, they leave them behind enemy lines fighting for their lives against a beast that wants nothing more than to suck the livelihood and humanity out of them before returning them back into society, if they are released at all. I don't say this to negate the actions of the underdeveloped human beings, which led to their criminal behavior and imprisonment in the first

1

place. However, we have to accept the harsh reality that prison was not *designed* with the intent to correct or rehabilitate human behavior. It in fact does the opposite. Prisons are nothing but a *temporary* and inadequate fix which makes millions of dollars off of Black and Brown communities. In the last 20 years thousands of schools have been closed in Black and Brown communities across this nation, especially in the City of Detroit which has heavily contributed to the 2.5 million people incarcerated in amerikkka. It costs close to $40,000 per year to house/storage a prisoner and between $7,000 and $8,000 per year to educate a student. From those numbers it is quite obvious that amerikkka the great, would rather incarcerate than educate.

I was released from prison on January 3, 2001 and was seriously tempted to kiss the ground! After having served nearly a decade behind prison walls, just having the ability to step foot onto the pavement unrestricted, felt like a luxury. Although I was extremely happy to be out, I was overwhelmed with the thought of returning home. It had been so long since I had been there and I had no idea what life would be like. While I was in deep thought on the Greyhound bus, I noticed this nice looking woman eyeballing me. I could tell by the way that she gazed at me that she was interested. So, it didn't take long for me to make my way back to her seat to see what my "game" was like after 9 years. She could tell by my beige khaki outfit and black shoes that I was just released from prison but, that didn't deter her from looking at me like a breath of fresh air. It became quite obvious that she was ready to breathe in all of me. So, after a little small talk we were locked and loaded, kissing and touching wherever. Even though I was open to doing a lot more exploring, even in public, she held her composure but I was like a male dog in heat.

As the Greyhound bus approached Detroit, my mind began to focus on my financial shit-uation. It was at that very moment that I realized that the only thing that was going to separate me from a bum on the street, was the family support I would be receiving. It became clear to me that I had been released back into society to face a loaded gun wherever I went. Even though I had my GED I knew that wasn't going to be sufficient enough to secure a job, because my skill level was minimal at best. I recognized more than anything that I would have to rely on my survival skills in order to maintain early on.

2

Before former Michigan Governor John Engler left office, his administration eliminated all of the college and trade programs which contributed to enhancing the skill level of many prisoners before their release. The programs his establishment eliminated were created to make prisoners more marketable and to help them to make successful transitions back into society. That decision by the Governor's office ensured that the Michigan Department of Corruptions/Corrections (MDOC) would either be honing career criminals or sending Black and Brown men to early graves after being released. Prisoners were leaving only to return within 6 months or die from gunfire because they were trying to catch up on what they had missed out on while incarcerated. His negligent actions further compounded many of the social challenges we were already faced with.

To be honest when the Greyhound bus arrived in Detroit, I was scared shitless. As I exited the bus, I recognized that wherever I went, I would face the harsh reality of either going back for some dumb shit or getting killed for some dumb shit. There was no blueprint for making a successful transition back into society. The blueprint that did exist as perpetuated by the mass media was only of men and women re-offending daily by engaging back into their criminal behavior. Even though there were numerous examples of men and women who had made successful transitions back into society, the mass media never told their stories.

My lil' sister Julia picked me up from the bus station and I had her take me to meet my parole officer, which was right across the street on 6th and Howard near downtown Detroit. She was a short, middle aged, well built Black woman who had a serious authority complex. She conveyed to me that until I found a job I would have to report to her once a week. Before I left her office she expressed to me that I should "watch the women out here".

My mama was staying in the Diggs Projects which were located across the street from the old youth home on East Warren and I-75 express way. She was living there temporarily while our house was being renovated because of lead. When I saw my mama I noticed something different about her. She was glowing with Black beauty. My sister had conveyed to me that she had not been drinking and I could tell. When my mama would drink her skin complexion would immediately change and she would look worn down. It felt good inside to see my mama looking

3

like her old self. After she gave me a big mama hug, she told me that my son DeAngelo was staying with one of his aunts on the eastside of Detroit and I would have to wait on my sister Rachelle to take me over there. He had been living with his mama's mother since she was shot and killed at a party when he was two years old. He was giving his grandmama pure hell and was only eight.

After his mama died, he was the apple of everybody's eye at his grandmama's house for about the first year. Unfortunately for my son, soon after that his aunts began having their own children and his grandmama had a baby right before him and right after him. So at the end of the day, I know that on many days and nights he came up short on being caressed and loved because they were too busy loving their own babies. That was one of the reasons why my mama always wanted him to stay with her. At her house my son could get all the attention he needed.

While I waited on my sister Rachelle to come and take me to visit my son, I had my sister Julia drive me to my neighborhood Zone 8. As we drove through Zone 8; the place I loved so much and was ready to die to defend its honor, I noticed it had been reduced to a ghost town. Actually it had always been a ghost town, but this time I was looking at my neighborhood through the eyes of *life* instead of through the eyes of *death*. Zone 8 like so many other Detroit neighborhoods, had suffered from years of social, political, educational, cultural and economical neglect which manufactured neglectful human beings. Many of the elected officials, business folks and clergymen saw the need to beautify downtown Detroit while turning a blind eye to the inner city neighborhoods, neglecting to recognize that the foundation of any city is its neighborhoods. When they failed to invest in the neighborhoods, they did their city and their greatest resource, its people, a huge disservice. We cannot have a *strong* city without having *strong* neighborhoods! I look at the blight, abandoned buildings and empty lots in Detroit neighborhoods as a direct result of misappropriated funds, political/religious/community activist/non-profit corruption and a lack of vision by those who so desperately want to lead this city and its residents. The more than three decade's worth of abandoned buildings still standing in Detroit neighborhoods is an ironic metaphor for the heart of this great city, which continues to fight for survival after having been left to create beauty out of some ugly shit!

4

I visited with many of the elders who still resided in my neighborhood and had known me since I was a little redheaded boy running through their blocks fighting all the time. I was proud to return to them as a man who had transformed himself. I also visited one of the only men in my neighborhood who had tried to teach my friends and me the right way to make an honest dollar. His name was Ted. When I was younger, he had my friends and I remove some debris from his yard. After we removed all of the debris he gave us a couple of quarters each. Although we all appreciated the quarters he gave us, we were really only interested in going to the penny candy store to play the video games. The quarters definitely came in handy but we were allergic to hard work. So, after that we always made sure we avoided Ted and his hard work. The principles he was trying to teach us of being responsible and working hard just didn't register with the street mentalities that we were developing. More importantly, neither of us had strong men in our lives on a consistent basis to cultivate and reinforce the importance of hard work and discipline. So, by default we began to gravitate towards cutting corners to get what we wanted because that was the *code of the streets*.

I stopped by his house and thanked him for the lessons he attempted to teach me and my friends during our childhood. I had no way of knowing that during my visit with Ted, I would be put in the middle of a conflict between him and other people in the neighborhood. Ted had purchased many of the properties in my neighborhood and during the process had rubbed many people the wrong way but, I overstood both sides. Here was a man trying to implement positive and productive change in our neighborhood by contributing to helping it maintain the look of being a *neighborhood* and not a *'hood*. However, the process he took to implement the changes alienated him from his neighbors. Instead of being recognized as someone who wanted to transform the neighborhood for the positive, Ted was deemed an enemy because everybody thought that he thought he was better than them. This was a neighborhood that had not seen any significant changes done to it in about 20 years so the people who were surviving in it were subconsciously content with the neighborhood deteriorating into a 'hood. Although they wanted change like the next person, their conditions did not allow them to embrace it. None of them had any desire to live or raise their children in a *crime infested neighborhood* but, the reality is that their *outcry for change* had fallen on deaf ears causing them to adopt

5

the mentality of *survival of the fittest* within their decaying neighborhood.

It is only a matter of time before the struggle for survival in a decaying neighborhood causes the souls, minds, aspirations and actions of its residents to begin to display the decay that they have become *immune* to. Unfortunately, urban neighborhoods, especially in Detroit are *defeated* neighborhoods often manufacturing *defeated* human beings and the urban youth who reside in those neighborhoods display a state of *defeatism* in their behavior. This in turn contributes to the mindset of youth who view criminal behavior as recreation because they have no recreational centers to absorb their free time.

My lil' sister Julia took me to go see my lil' homie Scottie-Mack (TIP). He stood about 6 '4 or 6 '5, was well built and from his demeanor I could tell that he was making power moves in Zone 8. Scottie-Mack had come a long way from being the little mascot of the gang. He stood as a strong Zone 8 souljah honing his own Zone 8 souljahs who would do whatever he commanded of them. We shared a special bond because I was right there with him when he earned his Zone 8 stripes. I can recall vividly, the day he won his first fight against the lil' homie Bo-Pete. They were both about the same size but, Bo-Pete was about three years older. It was pretty much an even fight but Scottie-Mack refused to lose the fight after taking some pretty good blows from Bo-Pete. So, he did everything in his power to come out victorious. After that night Scottie-Mack had won the approval of many of the homies who had doubted his Zone 8 passion and was well on his way to becoming a Zone 8 souljah. Before I left his house he gave me some money and we took some pictures together. Unfortunately, I had no way of knowing that my homie's days were numbered.

When my homie Scotty-Mack was murdered, it rocked my neighborhood to the core because a lot of people were depending on him. It hit many of the lil' homies especially hard because he had been for many of them, their only provider. I didn't condone how he chose to live his life but, I overstood his decision and had more respect for him than I did for many of the so-called leaders in our community who were out of touch with the people. Being a leader is about meeting the people where they are at. It is about standing with the people. It is about organizing the people. It is about serving the people by being firmly rooted with the people in every way possible. If we are not doing that, then we will continue to allow an underdeveloped leadership to meet the needs of the people.

I also went to see my other lil' homie Stacks. He and Biggs had just finished weighing up some dope and when Biggs saw me he was like, "what up thug life?" I never realized that the shit we were doing back in the day had been deemed gangsta or thugging. We never verbally proclaimed that we were gangstas or thugs, even though we were doing gangsta and thug shit every day. The thug and gangsta shit we were doing was just a natural part of our lives.

I kicked it with Stacks for a minute and he conveyed to me that after all the homies had gotten locked up, that he had to get his weight up in order to represent Zone 8. He went on to tell me that it all started after the guys from across the Boulevard had put a classic ass whipping on him. After talking with Stacks and Biggs, I realized the type of effect Zone 8 was having on its residents during my incarceration. Both Stacks and Biggs had been non-combative members before I left the street and weren't active gang bangers, even though they both considered themselves Zone 8s. Biggs and I were around the same age and I never remember seeing him get into a fight. Although Biggs was not living the death-style I led before prison, we were always cool because he was real down to earth.

Everybody that lived in the Zone or grew up there was considered a Zone 8 by default. However, not everyone was an active Zone 8 member charged with the duty to rep our neighborhood and gang wherever they went. The non-combative members eventually became full dedicated members after being jumped or attacked by a rival neighborhood or gang. Those members from rival gangs or neighborhoods did not take into consideration the difference between combatants and non-combatants. All they saw was a potential enemy and dealt with them as such. That process operated as the ritual for recruiting new members to fill up our Zone 8 ranks as well as the ranks of our rivals.

When the evening finally arrived, my sister Rachelle came and took me to see my son DeAngelo. I was super excited to see him because it would only be my second time seeing him in the eight years he had been in the world. When I walked into his aunt's house, I could see the excitement in his eyes from seeing me as well. I thanked his aunt for taking him into her home and she conveyed to me that he was doing much better in school since he had moved in. I then took my son to the side and expressed to him that I was going to allow him to stay at his aunt's house until school was out, which would be in a couple of months. I recognized that my son needed stability and I didn't want to disrupt his life by uprooting him and destroying the consistency he had become accustomed to. I wasn't on no ego trip, coming home demanding that because I was his daddy, he needed to stay with me. I appreciated what his mother's family as well as mine had done for my son while I was incarcerated and after his mother was killed. Plus, I wanted to establish some foundation for my life by finding a job and getting acclimated back into society before taking on the responsibility of being a full-time parent. I rationalized that removing my son from their custody at that moment would have been negligent on my part, so I didn't. Before I left his aunt's house my son asked me if he could grow braids like me and I said yes.

A couple of days went by and I received a phone call from my son's uncle telling me that I could come and get him, that all his shit would be packed up and that he would be waiting on me. My son's desire to be with me was so great that he began to act out in school and around the house, which made his uncle, feel disrespected. The root of his displeasure with my son was that he had welcomed him into his house and treated him like his own son but now all of a sudden, my son wanted his daddy. Out of his frustration with my son, he whipped him butt naked. My mama pleaded with me not to go over to his house and do anything crazy and it took all the strength in my body to control my anger. Luckily, my better judgment prevailed. When I got there my son was waiting on me. I retrieved his clothes and we left.

When I went to prison, both of my sisters were little girls. When I came home, they stood in front of me as grown women, with my sister Rachelle being a proud mother. My sisters and I loved each other deeply, but the reality was that incarceration had put a strain on our relationship. During my nine years of imprisonment, I received six visits from my family members. Only two of those visits were from my mother because it was too painful for her to see me locked up like an animal. We visited only once as a whole family. Sure, my sisters would have liked to visit more often, but they lacked stable transportation like so many other family members. This prevented them from driving thousands of miles through klu klux klan territory which lent to the strong possibility that they could be lynched if their car broke down.

Also, many of the white supremacist guards and knee-grow guards would do everything in their power to discourage family members not to visit by degrading and dehumanizing them with searches in which they treated them like criminals. The only other ways to stay in touch with family members were via telephone and letters. Making collect calls was a catch 22 because the phone charges ranged from $8-$10 for only 15 minutes, which was extremely high. Although most families could not afford to accept the calls, they accepted them anyway putting their families under even greater financial strain out of desperation and love. Writing letters was also challenging because it exposed the harsh reality that many prisoners and the family members that they wrote to, were illiterate.

These harsh realities prevent prisoners from maintaining healthy communication with their family members. This is the untold story of mass incarceration in amerikkka, which plays a devastating role in the destruction of families because of the lack of meaningful contact between prisoners and their relatives. There are prisoners across this country who have gone decades without a visit from a loved one. Can you imagine the psychological and spiritual damage caused to that human being?!

After being home for about a week, my old partner Rob came and got me to hang with him. We took his youngest son to get his hair cut and we started playing chess up at the barbershop. While we were playing chess, a few more guys came in and asked if anyone was interested in playing a real hustlers game; shooting dice. Rob didn't hesitate to take the brothers up on their offer and engaged them in a street game of dice. While they were shooting dice, he and one of the guys started talking gangsta talk to each other. I sensed where their gangsta talk was heading and told him I was going to take his son out to the car. Before I could even get him buckled in, I saw a crowd of guys coming out of the barbershop attempting to keep Rob and the guy separated. A few of the guys brought the guy across the street where I was and he was going off like a mad man. I decided to walk over to him and let him know that we didn't want any trouble but, he responded by telling me to get my *bitch ass* out of his face. Before I knew it, I had hit him with a straight jab, knocking him to the ground. When Rob got into the car, he looked at me in disbelief because he couldn't believe I had knocked dude out with one jab.

I could see in Rob's eyes that the life of being a gangsta was taking a toll on him. I also recognized that he was attempting to bury his problems by drinking. Rob and his father had an estranged relationship so the only thing Rob knew was the streets. He had graduated from the streets with an A+ out of necessity. Despite being a helluva street guy, I knew that he secretly sought peaceful days and nights as a man, father and husband. Before he dropped me off at home he told me that he could tell that I wasn't the "same old Joe" and that I had his support.

The first sexual relationship I had after prison was with this woman name Tamika that used to write me while I was incarcerated. She had even started coming to visit me near the end of my incarceration. During that time she wanted a relationship with me, but I was reluctant to enter into a relationship with her because of my shit-uation. However, despite my circumstances she still wanted me to be her man so, against my better judgment; I decided to take her up on her offer. She began to write me and we would talk on the phone via the three-way occasionally. Then, all of a sudden I stopped hearing from her completely. After about 6 months had passed, I caught up with her via phone and noticed her hesitation to talk. I sensed that she may have gotten pregnant but did not want to volunteer that information to me. So, I asked her if she was and she said yes. I wasn't mad at her because I was aware that it was extremely hard to maintain a healthy relationship during a person's stint of incarceration. More importantly we never had a real relationship in the first place prior to my incarceration, besides having sex during our teens. Almost a year after that conversation, she got back in touch with me and once again brought up the notion of us being in a relationship. I immediately conveyed to her that we had gone down that road before, it didn't work and I wasn't interested in trying it again. I told her that we could however remain friends. We began corresponding and she also began to visit me and send me money.

Upon being released from prison she never separated from the idea that she wanted me to be her man and more importantly wanted me to move in with her and her son. She believed that the time and money that she volunteered entitled her to be my woman. I politely conveyed to her again that I had no interest in being her man or staying with her and her son. No matter what I said, she had already conjured up in her mind that I was her man and that I would love the idea of moving in with her and letting her take care of me. What she didn't realize was that I couldn't see myself being totally depended upon a woman, or any person for that matter, besides my mama. In my heart, if I would have allowed myself to entertain a relationship such as that, I would have felt like less than a man. The sad reality is that a lot of men leave prison and allow women to take care of them with no hesitation, only to abandon them after they get on their feet. These types of relationships are built on desperation as well as vulnerability between the man and woman. Many women have been messed over by multiple men and they look at certain men coming out of prison as a new start on life because many of them return home after long stints looking as though they have been preserved. Being physically fit from years of exercising, spiritually grounded from years of soul searching and mentally sound from years of reading and studying, makes them appear to be the *ideal* man. The men coming out of prison see many of these women as a foundation to stand on as they work to reintegrate themselves back into society. They admire the hard work, strength and determination many of these women display under incredible odds, which makes them appear to be the *ideal* woman. The harsh reality is that neither are good for each other because they are both still carrying garbage from their past which makes them *damaged goods*!

We eventually maintained a nice sexual relationship but, I also started sleeping with another woman name Kim who I learned had a crush on me. I had been gone nine years so I was trying to release all of my sexual frustration. Although, they were both fully aware of what was going on, I could sense that the Tamika who wanted me to be her man started having issues with me sleeping with both of them. She intensified her efforts to lock me down as her man and I continued to express to her that I wasn't interested. One day I was at my mama's house having sex with the other woman and the woman who wanted me to be her man showed up unannounced. She was at the front door banging like she was crazy. Even if I wanted to ignore her knocks I couldn't, because they were so loud. By the time I made it downstairs my great uncle had let her into the house. It was like she knew I was right in the middle of having sex so she ran upstairs to find the woman I was having sex with. I

11

immediately ran up the stairs behind her in order to prevent any fighting from occurring between them. Once I got up the stairs, I grabbed her and told her that she had to leave and she responded by swinging on me. I ducked her punch and immediately realized that she was trying to entice me to hit her. I refused to hit her but, all of a sudden she got her hand on the iron and tried to rearrange my face with it. I moved quickly enough to miss her swing and immediately rushed her and wrapped my arms around her. She wouldn't let the iron go for nothing in the world so I rationalized in my mind that I had two options to get the iron out of her hand. One option was to knock the shit out of her and the other was to bite her on the hand in order to get her to release it. I chose to bite her and was able to retrieve the iron from her. After I got the iron out of her hand, she stormed out of my mama's house. Kim never came out from hiding during the confrontation between us.

When my mama got home I explained to her what had happened and she immediately took me to the police station to make a police report. We figured she was out of her fucking mind and was going to result to doing some *snake in the grass* shit. When I called my parole officer to inform her of the shit-uation, Tamika had already called and lied to her by telling her that I had jumped on her. My parole officer told me we would deal with the shit-uation when I came in to report. I thought about not reporting and just going on the run, because I was already aware that my fate was sealed on going back to prison for being violated on some bullshit. I decided against running and faced my shit-uation like a *souljah*.

When I walked into my parole officer's office, it didn't take long for her to have the handcuffs put on me and she definitely wasn't trying to hear my side of the story. As far as she was concerned, it was out of her hands and into the hands of the parole board. *I was in a state of shock.* I had not been home 30 days after doing nine years and I was already on my way back for some bullshit! I attempted to make one last plea but, she responded by saying that she had warned me about the females out here. As I was being escorted from her office I was crying hysterically. They were tears of anger!

I was taken to the infamous Jackson State Prison located in Jackson, Michigan. It would be my first time ever doing time there. Jackson State Prison used to be considered the *Godfather* of all the prisons in the State of Michigan. It was known to have gun towers in the chow-hall and it had a reputation for prisoners stabbing other prisoners or guards at the drop of a hat. Also, there were numerous prisoners who had committed suicide because they were paralyzed with the fear of being housed in the infamous Jackson State Prison. They couldn't handle the thought of possibly being raped or constantly harassed every time they left their cells by other prisoners or guards.

When I arrived at Jackson State Prison it was under construction and they were eliminating the infamous 12 block and 4 block which were known to house some of the toughest prisoners in the state. As I was going through the intake, I was told that I had to take my breads down. I started to resist, but I was too demoralized to even put up a fight against my oppressors.

Once I settled in, I immediately wrote my father and a few other comrads to inform them of my unfortunate shit-uation. The news of me being back spread like wildfire! As I awaited my parole hearing, my days and nights were filled with nothing but anger. To add insult to injury, I learned after calling home that my mama took my return to prison extremely hard and had started drinking again. My sisters also informed me that Tamika demanded money not to testify at my parole hearing. I had my sister Rachelle contact my homie Rob to take care of the money demands that she had.

It seemed like it was taking forever for my parole hearing to come and I was beginning to lose hope. While I was out in the yard clearing my head, I ran into my big homie Duck from the Zone. He attempted to keep my spirits high by telling me that everything was going to work out in my favor. During some of the talks he tried to convince me to put my faith in Jesus and He would work everything out. If I had been dealing with some spiritual people, I probably would have thought about praying to God but, I knew I was dealing with beastly people that were out for my blood. He and his brother Big Skip (RIP) had been in the drug game for over 20 years, either selling it or using it. His brother Big Skip ultimately died from an overdose.

The strange thing about my parole violation was that there were a bunch of other guys in there for the same thing. Some of them would earn their freedom while others were found guilty of their violations.

13

Being back in prison taught me a valuable lesson about recidivism, which I had previously taken for granted. That lesson was that it was *extremely* easy to get caught up in some dumb shit and be sent back to prison. All it took was for somebody to call in and say they saw you doing something allegedly illegal or hanging with the wrong person. Or, if you were caught in the wrong place at the wrong time, you were on your way back to a cell. All were grounds for violation. When you are on parole and you are taken to the police station, ain't no posting bail. You are headed straight to the county jail. Being back on some bullshit educated me through my own shit-uaiton not to be so quick to condemn other guys who returned back to prison within six months. Until you know a person's struggle, you honestly can't make a sound judgment about it. More importantly, thousands of men and women who are released from prison every month face the harsh reality of returning immediately, because none of them were properly prepared to make a successful transition back into society in the first place. The recidivism rates across this country are rooted in the fact that it is a conflict of interest to prepare men and women not to return to prison.

When my court hearing finally arrived, the woman never showed up even though she didn't have to come to Jackson, Michigan. She could have attended a teleconference in Detroit. The white parole officer turned pink as hell in the face once he learned that she was a "no show". He decided right then and there to postpone my hearing another week instead of granting me freedom, which was the procedure after an accuser fails to show up for a court hearing. This decision was unheard of, but clearly demonstrated the beast's deep desire to keep me in their clutches.

While I waited on the next parole hearing I attended the Nation of Islam service to clear my head. While there I ran into this elder prisoner named Poncho X. He was back on a parole violation as well. At one point and time he was a prominent member of the Melanic Islamic Place of the Rising Sun; the religious organization my father joined as well as myself when I was in prison. It had been banned within the MDOC through its Security Threat Group policy in 1998. Through speaking with him I learned that he was a close comrad of my father who had also mentioned his name to me a few times via letters. We kicked it for a minute and wished each other the best in the name and spirit of *Nat Turner*.

14

When my hearing arrived the second time, the woman was still a "no show". So, the parole board had no choice but to grant me my freedom. It taught me an important lesson, which was that there is nothing like the vindictiveness of a scorn woman.

FINDING EMPLOYMENT

Chapter 2

When it finally dawned on me that my parole had been yanked from under me as quickly as I had gained it, I felt *demoralized*. Not only did I have to face the fact that I had been accused of assaulting a woman but, it would be the second time I was sent to prison for a crime I didn't' commit. This hit me like an upper cut, knocking the wind out of my lungs and leaving me both dazed and confused. Despite the fact that I was terrified, I was ready to face my fears like a prize fighter.

I didn't know where to begin after being released. My world had been shattered and I found it difficult to put the puzzle, which was now my life, back together. I felt like I was losing the battle of trying to become a responsible man and father which made me feel like I was losing a part of my soul. Before my release, all I could think about was proving my worth as a man and father, but nothing prepared me for the reality that the society I wanted to reintegrate back into would socially reject me every step of the way. That short month and a half that I found myself back in incarceration, had accomplished what the prison system had failed to do in the nine years that I was locked up previously, which was to *break me*. I felt like the world was crumbling around me. I had no money and no job and the prospect of getting either through legal means didn't seem possible. I could not even afford to buy my son a pair of gym shoes so; I was suffocating as a man and as a father because of my lack of financial stability. My mother and sisters were supporting me as much as they could, but at the end of the day, they had their own struggles to deal with. I began to feel like my struggles were becoming a burden on my family and the pressures on my shoulders were rapidly mounting against me.

A lack of strong family support for men and women who return home from prison makes the transition back into society much more difficult. That support takes on many different levels but has to be rooted in *tough love*. We already face an uphill battle because of the lack of support we receive from our parole officers, because many of them treat us as if we are some sort of *social cancer*. To make matters worse, many non-profit/faith based organizations are completely exploiting our

16

shit-uation by receiving millions of dollars, while we receive ineffective services which fail to meet our needs. The organizations are supposed to help us with basic needs such as retrieving our birth certificates and social security cards and they often fall short of even doing that. Many have been incarcerated so long that their immediate family members have either died or they've lost contact with them. So, they have no choice but to stay in one of these residential homes where they have four guys sleeping in the same room and up to between 10 and 15 men living in the same house. Sometimes these living conditions are worse than what they experienced in prison. The result of this counter-productive way of addressing the social challenges that many men and women who return home from prison face contributes to the high rate of recidivism. Between the first six months to one year after returning home from prison, they are likely to be solely reliant upon a family member. The support he or she receives that first six months to one year will play a crucial role in whether that person makes a successful transition back into society, dies or goes back to prison!

I started hitting the road every morning in effort to find a job. I filled out application after application only to be denied employment or to not hear anything back period. I was putting my best foot forward only to have doors slammed repeatedly in my face. When I initially came home I wanted to go to college because I felt like furthering my education would improve my skill level and put me in a better position to explore employment opportunities. Unfortunately, going to school became less of a priority when the reality set in that it would not immediately assist me with paying my bills or buying clothes for my son. I then considered picking up a trade which I felt would assist me with my desire to learn as well as teach me a skill set. So, I enrolled into Focus Hope's Machinist Training Institute. However, those educational dreams coupled with picking up a vocational skilled trade ultimately turned into a *social nightmare*. When my financial challenges became an even larger burden, I dropped out because they could not educate me rapidly enough to secure a job so that I could pay the bills.

One day I ran into a guy I was in prison with and he asked me if I wanted to ride around with him. I agreed since I didn't have anything up but, I had no idea that he was going to take me on a tour with him to check on his drugs houses. During the ride he began to ask me different questions. "How long you been home?" I responded by saying "only a

17

few months." He went on to ask the million dollar question. "What are you doing with yourself?" I knew it was a loaded question so I took a minute to answer it, even though it was quite obvious by my wardrobe that I was struggling. I responded by saying, "I am out here doing bad. I can't catch a break for nothing. I am doing the shit the right way by filling out job application after job application and attending many of these fake ass programs that ain't offering a nigga nothing but a conversation and some bus tickets." His response was quick and concise, "I've been home for a minute and one of my homies got me on my feet. I'm killing it out here baby and I could use a souljah like you Jo Jo!" He offered me a position on his drug team but I declined. "I appreciate the offer homie, but I'm cool." After that brief conversation we drove around further through Detroit and then went to get something to eat. When he dropped me off at my mom's house he gave me some money, an ounce of weed and a pistol. I was grateful for the money and even the ounce of weed because it would get me off craps for a minute but, I was skeptical as hell about the pistol. I made a few phone calls and sold the pistol quicker than I did the ounce of weed! I reasoned in my mind that the pistol had to have some "bodies" (people being shot) on it, because a guy in the street game just don't give his pistol away with such ease.

After I sold the ounce of weed, I had a couple hundred dollars in my pocket which included the money my homie gave me. I was somewhat feeling good about myself and then reality began to set in. *Here was a job that would not discriminate against me because of my felony and my lack of skill level.* Selling dope became my first employer and it took me from drowning in desperation to bathing in a little bit of hope. Since I didn't have a connection on purchasing my weed, I decided I would try my hand at selling heroin since many of my homies were selling it throughout my neighborhood. I had never sold heroin a day in my life although I had sold crack before. I pushed up on one of my little homies and explained to him what I wanted to do and that I needed his help. So, he gave me a gram of heroin out of love. Even though I had never sold heroin before, I had a cousin who had been using it for over 20 years, so he schooled me on how to sell it. I quickly learned it was a drug that you could up to triple your money on depending on how much of a "cut" you put on it with other medical drugs to stretch its value. I didn't have time for all that. My primary objective was to make some quick money so; I sold my dope "as is".

18

I was in a familiar *survival mentality* mode through selling drugs and operated strictly from the stand point of making money. I had no desire to make dope selling a career. All I cared about was being able to put food on my mama's table, clothes on my son's back and a few dollars in my pocket.

This is how it starts off for many drug dealers. The goal is to make some quick money but the more the person is entrenched in that mentality and environment, they evolve from petty hustlers into full time hustlers out for blood at the expense of people *by any means necessary*. Drug dealing becomes a sport of blood through a conquest of savages and predators as they become more rooted in the "Black Underworld." Drug dealers and other "illegal businesses" in the neighborhood broken down to their lowest dominator are nothing but "illegal capitalist" applying the same principles of exploitation at its highest degree. Capitalism (amerikkka's economical system) is nothing but the exploitation of human beings by a few human beings. The sad thing is that the drug dealers don't even know that they are imitating the real capitalists and imperialists that not only run this country, but this world through greed, exploitation and oppression.

Drug dealers imitate imperialist behavior through their conquest of neighborhoods. By setting up drug spots and trap houses which ultimately *wreak havoc and devour* neighborhoods, they deteriorate the people who are struggling to survive the underdeveloped behavior which eats at the humanity of everybody in the neighborhood. The value of the property in the neighborhood depreciates and vicious acts of violence create *warzones*. The underdeveloped behavior which begins to govern the neighborhoods, sucks the life out of the people and reduces the neighborhood to a 'hood which becomes a territory resembling a third world country full of people who begin to take pride in or become immune to surviving in a *crime infested* community. By imitating this capitalist/imperialist culture or extreme individualism, drug dealers contribute to keeping neighborhoods at the bottom, while the real capitalists and imperialists profit off of our exploitation and oppression through the means of incarceration. The "Black Underworld" is nothing but a "bastard version" of capitalism/imperialism!

Many guys who engage in the "Black Underworld" start off with some level of a code of ethics and follow many strict unwritten rules. But as they make money and acquire power as a result of that money, it attracts a multitude of beautiful women and materialistic gains (fancy cars, expensive clothing, etc.). All this speaks to the *'hood rich* status they have achieved through their drug occupation. After their new found *baller* (having money and 'hood fame) status has been obtained, the code of ethics and unwritten rules get thrown out the window. Guys start selling dope around schools, having sex with their partners' girlfriends or sisters, setting guys up to be robbed or killed and childhood friends turn into enemies over women and money because their desire to be the *man* eliminates their need for one another. In the business world this is called eliminating your competition! Upon being captured by the authorities for their drug operations, many of them post high bonds to be released, only to begin to sell drugs for the system literally. Every dime they make goes toward staying out of incarceration or seeking less time by paying high profile lawyers who make back deals with the prosecutors and judges.

The harsh reality in the 'hoods of Black ghettos across amerikkka is that the dope dealers operate like a "Ford Motor Company" or a "Burger King" supplying jobs to the less fortunate. Unfortunately, there aren't too many options for a person who has a felony and who suffers from *blatant social discrimination* as well as *social rejection*. Negligently, society continues to judge them based upon their past, thereby closing the door on their future. The first law of nature is self-perseveration, so many men and women who are boxed into criminal elements as "legal" employment jump at the opportunity. Although they recognize the ugly truth, which is the strong probability that they will either return back to prison or die violently, they take this route out of desperation. This decision offers some level of freedom from the prison of socially being discriminated against and socially rejected. When a person is buried in desperation their rational is centered on desperation and heavily influenced by an overdose of hopelessness and helplessness.

People on the outside looking in fail to overstand these social conditions. What they don't realize is that the neighborhoods in Detroit and other urban cities across amerikkka resemble *war torn countries* and people in these neighborhoods are surviving in "Third World" conditions. As Professor Carl S. Taylor at Michigan State University educates, "Urban Cities have been reduced to Third World Cities." At their height, Ford, GM and Chrysler the "Big 3", helped to develop a

20

thriving middle class in the City of Detroit. However, after the fall of the Big 3, the lack of jobs they once provided to those in the heart of the neighborhoods in Detroit, the introduction of heroin in the 70s and crack in the 80s, that thriving middle class begin to slowly evaporate. The Big 3 was eventually replaced with drug enterprises such as "YBI", "Pony Down", "Chambers Brothers", the "Curry Brothers", "Best Friends" and many others. Many of these drug enterprises received their drugs directly from the police. That once proud middle class was reduced to the poor class and the poor class was reduced to scavengers. The capitalist economic system killed the Big 3 because it is a system that thrives on sucking the blood out of its prey and then it ultimately turns on itself. Any system that is pro-individualism cannot be good for the whole because it makes its mark off of exploiting the whole. The ruling class thrives on exploiting the middle class, the middle class thrives on exploiting the poor class and the poor class thrives on exploiting each other. Those of us, who have been locked out of mainstream society as a way to provide for our families, find ourselves gravitating toward the subculture of the streets, i.e. selling drugs, robbing, prostitution etc. In order to provide for ourselves and our families we engage in this bastard version of capitalism, not even realizing that we are participating in our own demise. The goal of this subculture is to suck the life out of the neighborhoods and turn them into deplorable 'hoods.

It wasn't long before I realized that selling drugs wasn't working out for me. Even though I was doing my street thing, I was attempting to apply my "liberation principles" to individuals that just weren't trying to hear it. I was losing more than I was profiting because I was too busy trying to save everybody's souls. After I had sold the rest of the dope I had gotten from my other homie, my big homie Donnie (TIP) gave me a gram of dope out of love. Donnie had been selling dope since I was knee high. Soon after he gave it to me, I ran into my lil' homie "B-Mo" from the Zone and he began to tell me how his drug addicted mama had stolen all of his dope and money out of his drug spot. I felt sorry for "B-Mo" and ultimately gave him the gram of dope because I figured he needed it more than I did.

Within a few days of quitting my dope selling job, I was heavily pondering what I was going to do for employment. While out with my cousin Donna, I ran into a guy I was incarcerated with and he told me he was working for a landscaping company that was hiring out in Dearborn,

21

Michigan. Because of my connection to him I was hired in and I permanently quit selling drugs, no matter how bad things got for me. When I looked into the mirror I didn't like what I saw. I overstood my actions and decided that I would never try to justify them. I made a commitment to take full responsibility for my actions and was glad to be granted an opportunity to correct my behavior while reaffirming my oath to make it despite the many odds I would continue to face. I realized that I had come too far to throw in the towel so easily. It took reflecting on who I had transformed into while in prison and the mission I had come home with. At times the struggles I encountered kicked my ass and literally knocked the wind out of my sail but I had never been a quitter and was one hell of a fighter! So, I fought to keep my head above water despite the odds against me! Yes, I've lost a few battles but the objective was to win the war and there was a lot of fight left in me. I reasoned that the best souljahs have fallen down on the battlefield so it wasn't about falling down; it was about picking myself up and continuing to fight until I had no fight left! I began to reflect on an important lesson my father had shared with me while we were both in prison during one of our building sessions. He taught me that the greatest battle I would ever fight would be the war within myself and that the outcome of my internal battle would determine how I engaged in my external battles. I recognized that the battle I had to fight was the battle to restore my self-worth. This process began by recognizing that my value as a human being was greater than my circumstance. I had to focus on controlling my circumstances and not letting my circumstances control me. I was ultimately able to do that by enduring my struggles. Through endurance I would put myself in a position to rise above them. This inspired me to fight this uphill battle of becoming a productive man and father.

BECOMING A MAN

Chapter 3

I finally obtained what was considered a legitimate job with Kelly Services, a temporary "temp" agency. After working there for a minute, I would discover that the only jobs that were available for felons were with different temp agencies and that they were profiting like hell off of us. To make it even more blunt, they were "pimping us like 90 going north". They were making a profit equal to what each felon was paid whether the organizations they loaned us out to retained us or not. Felons are a labor class in amerikkka with no proper representation and are treated as a permanent underclass; openly exploited by businesses, churches and non-profits. Because of these conditions, many of us feel like the voiceless and faceless human beings of amerikkka so we rarely think about arguing or challenging our exploitive conditions. We are caught in a catch-22 shit-uation, either we work for modern day slave wages or we don't work at all.

It was a win, win shit-uation for the temp agencies to employ us, while we lost on every end. Many of the them were protected through the federal government bonding program, which was insurance in case one of us relapsed and stole or broke something on the job. The jobs that employed us through these temp agencies became the new plantations with only one purpose in mind; work the shit out of us! Not to mention the instances where there were back door deals cut in order to get us hired, with the main purpose of them receiving millions of dollars. Unfortunately, none of this changed the fact that many still felt it was necessary to lie on their applications about not having a felony due to the open discrimination we often faced. Even with the bonding programs and other programs that were supposed to secure our employment, we found ourselves walking on eggshells because we would be fired once they found out one of us lied about our felony record. What is even more disturbing, is that after terminating one of us, they would continue to collect money for hiring us. Those of us that did not lie on our applications about having a felony were laid off right before our 90 days were up after being lead to believe we would be hired in as full-time workers. "Even though we like your work ethic and appreciate you as a worker, unfortunately we have no room for you!" This is basically how the conversation went with a supervisor. Sure, many of us knew the outcome before it happened because we had all seen or heard about it happening before. We were just hoping it would be different for us. Unfortunately, we had to face the harsh reality that it was not. This is just one of the examples of open discrimination formerly incarcerated individuals face when it comes down to seeking employment. The inability to secure a permanent job which offers medical insurance for you and your family, adds to the hopeless and helpless feelings that plague former prisoners. Our social reality is to work a slave's wage in a slave-like environment or don't work at all!

There are so many men and women returning home from prison each month, that we make up a *whole new social class* in amerikkka. We are *labeled* as ex-offenders, felons or returning citizens which permanently cements us as *third class citizens* who are openly discriminated against and exploited. This discrimination *boxes* us into exploring underdeveloped behavior or what society deems as criminal behavior, as a means to provide for ourselves and our families. We are forced to work whatever jobs become available, because most companies, although they claim to be equal opportunity employers, refuse to hire us. As a result, many of us are unable to obtain jobs and resort back to what we know best, criminal behavior. Then, without providing all the elements of their stories, the media bashes the individuals in a barrage of negative publicity. They will never ask the fundamental questions. Why wasn't this person *prepared* to make a successful transition back into society? Is it the fault of the man or the woman or the fault of the prison administration? If a man or woman has been incarcerated for 5 to 20 years and the only thing that has happened in their life over that time is incarceration, why would you expect their behavior to be changed?! Prisons were not *designed* to correct human behavior. This is evident in the thousands of men and women who come home just to find themselves indulging in the same behavior that lead them to prison in the first place.

Society has sold us on the lie that prisons are a place that nurtures rehabilitation, but that is far from the fucking truth! Prison is an *animalistic environment* that mirrors the underdeveloped elements within the street culture. Those elements are drugs, prostitution, extortion, rape, violence, manipulation, gambling and anything else you can think of. However, the *untold story* of these underdeveloped elements is that the

24

prison administration and the prison guards are at the heart of it. *Nothing goes on in prison without the administration and guards knowing about it.* They *control* the fucking prison environment and they allow, as well as encourage, many of these behaviors. These conditions allow them to gain stronger control over the prison population, while at the same time making a profit by looking the other way when a prisoner is stabbed or raped. They also benefit from the drugs that they bring in for prisoners to sell.

The only type of rehabilitation that is taking place in prison is from the men and women who are taking their destiny into their hands to atone and redeem themselves and come out a better human being. *My father rehabilitated me in prison.* If it were left up to prison I would still be a gang banger! *If my father had not redeemed himself, I wouldn't be a redeemed man. If my father had not transformed himself, I would not be a transformed man.* My father taught me the lessons of redemption and transformation, which I embraced internally. Prison didn't change me! It was new information that changed me! It was new information that challenged me to stop looking at the world through the eyes of an underdeveloped human being, encouraged me to look at the world through the eyes of a human being and demanded me to behave like a human being!

When you look at the *new social class* of people who return home from prison, when I first came there were no one lobbying on behalf of us on a national level, which allow us to continue to be fucked over inside of prisons as well as on the outside. *Every human being should have the right to work.* Failure to provide employment opportunities for every human being is a social crime that is being committed everyday is this fucking country.

I worked my ass off at my job because I was always looking over my shoulder wondering when I would hear somebody come and tell me I was *fired.* When you are an ex-prisoner, you are mentally trained/conditioned to expect the worst and hope for the best. I took pride in being the first person to arrive at work and the last person to leave everyday. I did everything I could to prove my work ethic. I even did extra work. I did whatever it took!

While I was working with the temp agency, my cousin Kevin came home and I got him hired in. On our lunch breaks we used to talk about the time we spent together at the prison in Coldwater, Michigan. While Kevin was in Coldwater with me, he would joke about how he could out exercise me and one of my partners. So, when he finally brought his ass into the weight pit, we worked the shit out of his ass. He never came into the weight pit again to workout with us. It was good for my soul to souljah with my cousin, because my closest friends were my books in prison. He was real receptive to my change and even began to read some of the books from my library.

Kevin was a *gorilla* in the streets, and when he fell off the deep end he played for keeps. He had defied death many times while exploring his dark side. Even though he continued to escape death, the beast (prison) would always catch him. That is a common reality for many of us who are caught up in the street life thinking we can *out slick* the prison system. Even when we thought we were winning, we were actually losing because the outcome was always the same. We were either dying or going to prison at the cost of destroying our communities through underdeveloped behavior and criminality, while at the same time destroying our own humanity! The criminal behavior we found ourselves engaging in contributed to the genocide of our community through our act of being genocidal soldiers. Unfortunately, the movie we continued to watch and emulate would end with us either returning to prison or dying.

While my cousin was working with me, he demonstrated the same type of attitude that I did. He busted his ass in order to prove his work ethic. Demonstrating that he was a dependable worker paid off and he was rewarded by being hired in as a full time employee. Unfortunately, after only being hired in for a few weeks, they did a back ground check and found out that he had been incarcerated. They fired him on the spot! All that hard work he had done, didn't count for shit! To them he was a "felon/ex-offender" and proved his criminal intent by lying on his application. The rest of the week I worked on pins and needles wondering if I would be fired next. The reality was as long as I didn't seek full-time employment I was fine.

Being employed afforded me the opportunity to move from living with my mama to upstairs from her and I began to pay her rent once a month. My son stayed downstairs with my mama. It was at this time that I realized that I was relating to my son as more of a big brother/big homie than a father. One day when he was in the neighborhood over one of his friend's houses playing, I went to pick him up. While we were driving through the neighborhood, he blurted out, "that is the guy that was picking on me." Before I knew it, I had pulled over and he had jumped out of the car to fight the boy. It hit me like a ton of bricks that I had just did a "drive-down" with my son without hesitation! This incident educated me that my son was looking for "Jo-Jo" to come home and not "Yusef". I fed right into it because I lacked parenting skills. Sure, I had the desire to come home and be a father to my son, but I had no clue of how to do it. Because I had only seen my son once before I came home from prison, we did not have the opportunity to bond and prison did not offer me any parenting skills. Shit, they gave less than a fuck whether I had acquired the skills or knowledge to raise my son to be a productive member of society! All they cared about was creating a system which would have me and many others returning to prison in order to keep the prison guards employed. I eventually broke the fight up between the boy and my son and we drove home. I failed to realize that my lack of parenting skills would have a negative impact on me and my son's relationship. Unfortunately, I would find that out the hard way.

Living on my own not only taught me how to pay bills, but it taught me how to be *responsible*. I was completely ignorant to this and had it not been for staying with my mama, I would have been evicted for being irresponsible. I had no concept of managing and budgeting money and it showed after I would blow my money on bullshit and have nothing to show for it. During this period I officially started dating Kim from the neighborhood. I learned she developed a crush on me after looking at some of the pictures I sent home. Shortly after we began dating, I moved her in with me. Even though we claimed to be in love with each other, the only thing I actually loved was the sex.

One day while I was at work, a white guy I was cool with asked me to go to a bar with him. I had been home about four months and had not been out yet so, the idea of going out was very tempting to me. After weighing the pros and cons, I decided to go. The bar was Downriver, outside of Detroit in a predominately white community. I asked him if it was going to be cool for me to go to this bar and he replied confidently,

"Yes!" I was very apprehensive about hanging out in an all white community being Black, but decided to go against my better judgment.

We arrived around 11:30 PM and I sat there for about 30 minutes checking out the surroundings. I only noticed two other Black people in the bar besides myself. Surprisingly, they were partying like they were right at home among a packed room full of white folks. I grabbed my beer and stood beside the stage listening to the band. A young white female began to hold a conversation with me explaining that the drummer was her boyfriend. Before I could respond, a drunk white guy came out of nowhere and stood right in front of me with his cheek so close to my face that I could have kissed him if I wanted to. I immediately thought to myself, "I better get the fuck on before I have to fuck somebody up." I walked outside and saw the guy that I came with talking to another drunk white guy. "Dude lets go before I have to fuck somebody up", I said. He responded by asking me what was wrong. Before I could explain what happened, the guy who stood in front of me came running outside with a pool stick and a bunch of people were following behind him trying to calm him down. I immediately jumped into attack mode. I took my beer bottle and busted it against the brick wall turning it into a weapon. The first guy to run up on me was the drunk guy who was talking to the guy I came with. I didn't have time to figure out why he was approaching me, so I took my weapon and stuck him in the face. I stuck the next guy that ran up on me as well. After that, I took off running like my name was Jessie Owens. I realized while I was running that I had no fucking idea where I was running to. It was about one o'clock in the morning and I had no means to contact anybody. Even though I was running from *danger*, I reasoned in my mind that I was probably running to *greater danger* in an all white neighborhood and setting myself up to possibly get *lynched*. So, I decided to face my danger head on. I turned around and ran straight to the white mob that was chasing after me and my weapon and I went to work. Before they could get the best of me, the guy I came with drove his car into the crowd, I jumped in and we made our escape to Detroit.

I was mad as hell after the brawl with the white mob and I didn't say shit during the entire ride home. During my anger I thought to myself, "when we get to my house I should beat the shit out of his ass." I ultimately decided against it because I reasoned that I couldn't blame him for the racist acts of other white people. When I went to work that

Monday, I started having a conversation with a Black guy from River Rouge, another city outside of Detroit. River Rouge has a large Black population but is also a part of Downriver. He began to tell me about a brawl that happened at a Downriver bar over the weekend. One of the white guys who were part of the white mob had told him about it. He went on to tell me that one of the white guys got stabbed in the mouth and had to get like 50 stitches. "They said the Black dude they was fighting was on some super nigga shit…He just ran and started fighting the whole fucking crowd by his fucking self!" I responded by saying, "that will teach them about fucking with a Black person!"

Amerikkka's northern cities are as *segregated* as the racist south was almost 60 years ago, or should I say still is today, with Detroit being one of the *biggest* segregated cities in amerikkka. The illusion of racial progress and racial equality in this country is a fucking joke, because at the core of amerikkka's foundation is *white supremacy*. There has never been an even playing field for the indigenous people, which this country truly belongs to. It was snatched from them through a declaration of war which justified the warmongers acts through "Manifested Destiny." Afrikans were forcefully brought to this country through conquest; and their sweat, tears and blood is what fertilized the soil of this country. The foundation of which amerikkka stands on was establish through colonization, which empowered her to become a great empire following in the footsteps of the Romans. Her history is written in the blood of other nations! Her language is that of conquest, by any means necessary! Her religion is that all must submit to her! Her culture is that of violence! Her education is that white is pure and everything else is impure! Many of her grandchildren and great grandchildren bath in this white supremacy mentality as way of life!

The migration of southern Blacks to northern cities in amerikkka, exposed the northern racism of whites that fell under the radar. Because the brutality was not as open in the north as the brutality Blacks were facing daily by southern whites, the appearance was that things were different or considered better in *white north*. In 1943, here in Detroit, we experienced the first of two major "race riots/rebellions." The race riot in 1943 started on the small island in Downtown Detroit called, Belle Isle. The tension between Blacks and whites over an altercation escalated into a three day "race riot" which ultimately led to the federal troops being called in. When the smoke cleared after the three

29

days of rioting, 35 people were killed, 25 of which were Black and it was reported that over 600 people were injured, the majority Black as well and close to 2000 people were arrested. The majority of them were also Black.

After the arrival of Blacks to northern cities in inordinate numbers, northern whites did not disappoint in demonstrating their racist attitudes towards their new Black neighbors. They burned crosses in their yards and exploited Blacks through the northern practice of "Blockbusting", where white home owners would sell their homes below market value. Black folks were forced to buy the homes at a higher-than-market price from white real estate companies. Not to mention that many of the grocery stores sold bad food to poor Black families daily. The influx of more and more Black people migrating to northern cities for job opportunities sparked a trend of more and more white people moving out. White flight became the *social movement* to deal with Black people's quest for equality in education and job opportunities. That equality never came into fruition because Black people found themselves facing the same wretched social and educational conditions that they faced down south with a northern white racist flavor.

This gave birth to popular Black neighborhoods such as "Black Bottom" in Detroit in the 1950s. Black Bottom became a beacon of social, cultural, educational and economical hope for Black folks. It spoke to the history of Black people in amerikkka, which was developing and creating beauty out of some ugly racist conditions! In Black Bottom, many successful Black-owned businesses, social institutions and night clubs were able to sustain a healthy Black community and were independent of the larger white racist society. This successful Black community became a target for what was deemed as an "urban renewal project." Black Bottom was demolished and was replaced by the Chrysler Freeway (Interstate 75) and Lafayette Park, a residential development designed by Mies van der Rohe. This new expressway and park took high priority over Black life. Black people were forced to relocate to other parts of Detroit as if they didn't matter, which is the common theme of amerikkka. Unfortunately, Black Bottom is a forgotten history of Detroit whose Black reliance and self-determination were destroyed and are rarely spoken of.

Detroit is a city that became 85% Black by *default* and the surrounding cities became 85% white as well as other nationalities by *design*. In order to further overstand the social, economical, educational and political plight which has been imposed on Detroit, examine the *embargo* that amerikkka has *imposed* on Cuba over 60 years. The same type of *embargo* has been *imposed* on Detroit by the surrounding white suburban cities who *engage in unfair treatment of Detroit*. These white neighboring cities are openly engaging in institutional racism as well as open racist acts towards all of their neighboring Black cities. Examples of these neighboring cities are Detroit, Benton Harbor and Highland Park, etc. Can you imagine Coleman A. Young, who was elected the first Black Mayor of Detroit in 1974 attending a political gathering here in the State of Michigan with other politicians who were more than likely all white? You can just about guarantee that he had to deal with the white "good ole boy" network. Moving into the 80s, 90s and even the 2000s we have witnessed the tragedy of Black politicians openly betraying the people they were elected to serve by going out for self and selling Detroit out to the highest bidders. Many of them openly choose to cater to the white elite by developing "Downtown" Detroit for white people's enjoyment, while neglecting the Detroit neighborhoods, leaving Black people to suffer in them. The *foundation* of any city is it's neighborhoods and failure to invest in those neighborhoods is a complete betrayal and *jab* at the heart of the city. When resources stopped making their way to the neighborhoods, the neighborhoods began to *dry* up like a river and the people began to prescribe to a *survival of the fittest mentality*. We can't have a strong Detroit without strong neighborhoods. *It is impossible!* In order for Detroit to make a strong come back, we have to *re-spirit* the people with a fresh commitment to each other that is stronger than anything materialistic. More importantly, we need to usher in new leadership (politically, religiously, educationally, business and community wise) who overstand this and are willing to work to cultivate their services by serving the people.

During this period, my adjustment to being home was progressing. My daily routine consisted of going to work and then afterwards walking the my neighborhood like I was on a prison yard. I treated my house like my prison cell. Once I was done with my activities for the day, I reported to my house and called it a day. I had serious issues of anti-social behavior so, when I was confined to my house, I felt the most comfortable. I know this sounds daunting, but the harsh reality

31

is that I had to operate from this process if I was going to make a successful transition back into society. Yes, I was *institutionalized*! However, we are all *institutionalized by something!* Amerikkka is a big ass institution which teaches us what to think instead of how to think!

Every person who returns home from prison is a changed person. Mentally and spiritually we have been further *damaged* in a way that makes it difficult to behave like human beings. Our sense of humanity has been damaged from being forced to survive in *animinalistic environments* which reduced us to *animalistic behavior* in order to survive in the concrete jungle.

My adjustment to my neighborhood was taking on a different type of connotation. Since I was operating from a strict regiment as if I was in prison, many of the people in my neighborhood thought I was acting funny. In reality, I was acting *funny*. It was necessary that I duplicate the controlled environment that I was used to functioning in while I was in prison in order to cope with the pressures I faced on a day to day basis. If I hadn't developed that survival technique, I would have caved in. Even though I was in the neighborhood I grew up in, I felt like a *stranger* after being snatched away for 9 years. There were many new homies holding down the block earning their thug stripes through different acts of violence and they gave less than a damn who I was. They saw me as a potential opportunity to earn a major "hood status" by knocking off someone who was considered an *O.G.* (Original Gangsta). I refused to go out like that! I heard too many stories of guys coming home from prison and returning to their neighborhoods only to be killed. They were trying to play catch up in the street game and felt like many of the young homies owed them something. Many of the young homies made it clear that they didn't see things the same way and supplied them with some hot lead (bullets).

This is a social phenomenon that is rarely talked about in the neighborhoods. The young homies are *inheriting* the obligation to be like the big homies, which are at the core of the destruction of our communities continuing to recycle a death-style culture amongst our youth. Many of the young homies grow up in the shadow of the big homies and can't wait to step into their shoes at all costs in order to prove their thug and gangsta worth by any means necessary. With each new generation, thugs and gangstas usher in a mentality that is more deadly than the previous one. This *mentality* is connected to greed, violence and community destruction. In their *appetite* for destruction, many of the young homies live for the opportunity to make a name for themselves by knocking off one of the big homies. Accomplishing this feat writes them into "hood history" as officially being a "G" (Gansta). Everything after that is child's play, which is demonstrated in the ease of their community destruction. As long as we have absentee fathers, occasional fathers who lack productive fatherhood skills, a lack of strong male role models and a lack of fearless leadership with a concrete vision willing to challenge these young men and provide them a different model to emulate, they will continue to be *community predators* instead of *community protectors*.

WOMEN AND SEX

Chapter 4

On September 11, 2001, I went to work like everyone else. While my co-workers and I were in route to different landscaping jobs, vague reports of what was happening in New York were airing over the radio. After our lunch break, we drove to our last location, a Ford Motor Company building in Dearborn, Michigan. While we were working, we noticed droves of people leaving, but we were in the complete dark about all the foot traffic. Then we finally got the word that amerikkka was under attack and that the "Twin Towers" had been blown up. They also reported that certain buildings in the Metro Detroit area were on the list to be attacked as well. The building we were working at was being evacuated for safety reasons, but no one bothered to tell us. In my lifetime I've never felt more like a "slave" than I did at that very moment!

It was obvious that our lives didn't mean as much as the lives of the people who worked in the Ford Motor Company building. After all, we were human beings that had been convicted of a felony and sent to prison for irresponsible social behavior. This obviously made us expendable. When a judge sentences a person to prison, he/she proclaims in their courtroom that the person is being sent away to pay their debt to society. However, after several years, often decades of incarceration, they are released back into society only to realize that they are still paying on that debt. *Once you have been branded with a prison number, you become that prison number.* You have now been dehumanized at one of the highest levels because society no longer recognizes you as an individual but as a number. This number cements the fact that you will forever be indebted to a society that not only fears you, but writes you off as a menace. No matter your crime, whether alleged or factual, you will pay for your debt for the rest of your life.

Our supervisor eventually told us to pack up because we had finished the job. Even though many of us knew that our lives were potentially in danger, none of us had the balls to walk off the job site because our jobs were our livelihood.

Because of the political consciousness I had developed in prison, I overstood immediately what was happening in amerikkka. Malcolm X said it best when he said, "the chickens are coming home to roost!" The violence that amerikka had perpetuated on other countries over hundreds of years through *murder and mayhem* was coming back to bite her in her ass. Amerikkka's history is written in the blood of other countries through the murder of their people and the assassination of their leaders, with the goal of securing *white power*.

As a human being I wished death on no one and I am at a loss for words regarding all the people that were killed on 9-11! However, I would be negligent if I failed to point out that Black and Brown people in amerikkka were ground zero long before 9-11! Our body count is in the millions and it continues to be ignored. Amerikkka has no desire to help us. We are the illegitimate children that she has *disowned* and she seeks only to profit off of our misery. There have been gang wars that have existed with the "Crips" and "Bloods" in L.A. and the "Vice lords" and "Gangsta Disciples" in Chicago where the body count of Black and Brown people are in the hundreds of thousands from the 1970s until now. Amerikkka is supposedly committed to bringing peace to third world countries such as Iraq, Iran, Libya and Afghanistan, but she openly neglects the third world cities (urban cities) and third world neighborhoods (urban neighborhoods) that are in desperate need of peace right here in her own backyard. The blood of hundreds of thousands of Black and Brown bodies who have died as a result of gang wars here in amerikkka, are dripping from her hands because of her inability to see that Black and Brown people are worth saving. Instead, she has elected to view them only as a potential profit, making them expendable when they are no longer profitable.

I was amazed to see how patriotic so many Black people in this country were after 9-11. They donated millions of dollars to the survivors of 9-11, but some of these same Black people won't even donate a penny to save the life of another Black person. Black people in amerikkka still suffer from an *overdose of self-hatred* which impacts us to interact with each other from a negative stand point. Self-hatred is the step-child of white supremacy and it is imperative that we as Black people finally deal with self-hatred if we wish to create healthy households. Healthy households produce healthy schools; healthy social programs and healthy churches, which in turn create healthy human beings who develop healthy communities.

All of my hard work eventually paid off. Out of 25 temp services workers, I was the only one who was kept on the winter crew. I was excited about being rewarded for my work, because it was long overdue. I went from working on day shift to working on midnight shift, which was a slight pay increase. Unfortunately, my celebration would be short lived because the midnight shift was kicking my ass. I had never worked that shift before and my body never adjusted to it. I would get off work at 6AM and wouldn't fall asleep until around 11AM and be back up by 2PM to make it to work by 3PM. I would eventually be fired for falling asleep in the building. In hindsight, I believe being fired was actually a blessing in disguise because I had fallen asleep while driving the company truck a few times. I was very fortunate that I didn't end up in a fatal car accident, killing myself or someone else. Luckily, my income tax check arrived shortly after my termination, because it held me over until I found my next job.

During this period, my relationship was falling apart. In actuality, our relationship was never meant to sustain challenges because it was built on false pretenses. Kim was one of my little sister's friends who had developed a huge crush on me based upon a few pictures I had sent home. We had sex the same night my sister introduced us to each other and every night after that. Sex was the glue that held our relationship together.

As you can imagine, I was like a dog in heat that couldn't wait to get me some after being in prison for nine years and my sister's friend became my way to release all of my sexual frustration. I didn't know how to be with a woman in a romantic way, which would negatively impact our relationship and every other relationship I found myself in. When I went to prison I had just turned 19 but I was functioning more like a 13 year old. Prior to going to prison the few relationships I had were strictly physical. I had no mental concept of how to be with a woman besides "fucking the shit out of her." The *education* I received as a male in a sexist society was to deal with women from a physical stand point only.

36

One day I was at the CVS in my neighborhood located on the corner of Rosa Parks and West Grand Blvd when I noticed this light skinned and very thick beautiful woman. I approached her and introduced myself and she introduced herself as Faith. By the end of the conversation we exchanged numbers. Even though I was still in a relationship with my sister's friend, I had my eyes on something else and I was determined to explore her in every way possible. I eventually called her and asked her to go out with me and we ended up going out to the movies. When we left the movies I drove her through my neighborhood. She immediately told me that she was familiar with my neighborhood Zone 8 because her daughter's father was from there. So, I began to inquire about him. I learned that her daughter's father was a guy named Matthew who was the younger brother of my former rival B.J. from the neighborhood.

During our early conversations, Faith explained to me that she had three children by three different fathers and had not been in a serious relationship in a few years. She had her first child at 14, the second one at 15 and the last one at 20. Unfortunately, only one of her children's fathers was actively involved in helping her raise her children. Her oldest child's father had been incarcerated shortly after their child was born but expressed his desire to continue their relationship upon his release. However, after he was released, Faith informed him that she had moved on but welcomed his help in raising their son. Negligently, he responded by telling her that if she wasn't interested in being with him, he wasn't interested in being in his son's life. This is one of the tragedies of incarceration. There is nothing in place to *cultivate* the relationship between an incarcerated parent and a child. Statistics boldly tell us that the percentage is high for a child who has an incarcerated parent to drop out of school and more specifically, a male child is highly likely to follow his father to prison. What is alarming is that society has done nothing to proactively address these statistics besides talking about them. As I stated earlier, in the state of Michigan it costs close to $40,000 to warehouse a prisoner and between $7,000 and $8,000 to educate a student. This is how our society contributes to maintaining this permanent underclass of people who have been to prison. They anticipate that the children of the incarcerated will ultimately become their cellmates so they continue to build new prisons across this racist country.

37

During the early part of courting Faith, I had made a strong impression on her so she invited me over her house to meet her children and the rest of her family. Her youngest son, which was about four or five, took to me instantly. Since her children gave her their approval, she decided to be in a relationship with me. I was astonished by the fact that she suddenly wanted to be in a relationship because prior to me she had no desire to be in a one. I was in awe that this woman saw something in me that I didn't see in myself. Ultimately, the relationship I was in with my sister's friend came to an end when someone told her that they saw me kissing a woman at CVS.

One day my homie Li Li and I went over to Faith's house. I was inside the house chilling with her and her family when her daughter's father came over. When Matthew walked in the house and recognized me he looked as if he had just seen a ghost. It had been over 15 years since the last time he saw me and that experience was as enemies, not friends. By the look in his eyes, I knew he was wondering if his life was in danger. I immediately approached him and assured him that there was no beef between us.

The relationship between Faith and I was progressing nicely. She even helped me with my parenting skills through observing her parent her three children. Having a son that was around the same age as her son worked out as well, because they became *road dawgs*. Also, during this time, my son had signed up for a Black history contest at the Duffel Library and he asked me to help him write for it. He knew I was well versed in Black history and he wanted to win. The essay we wrote together was titled, "History is A Form of Appreciating Yourself" and he won second place for it. He also received a "Spirit of Detroit Award" from the Detroit City of Council. We wrote about the life of Carter G. Woodson, the founder of "Negro History Week", which was later, renamed "Black History Month" in the 1960s. He also founded the "Journal of Negro History", which was later renamed "The Journal of African American History" and wrote one of the most important books for Blacks in amerikkka, "The Mis-Education of the Negro".

Most men have issues with being involved in a relationship with a woman who has children by other men. I felt like if I had taken that attitude it would have been disrespectful to my own mother because Faith's life had mirrored my mother's life. I would have been walking in

38

the same shoes as the many men that treated my mother like she wasn't shit because she had children by other men. I treated Faith's children like my own children and she treated my son like her own. One day her daughter's father came up to me and conveyed to me that he thought I was a good man because I bought his daughter some clothes.

In society, women with multiple children are deemed as damaged goods by certain men. But what is never mentioned by these men is that women like Faith and my mother become damaged goods because of no good men who fuck over them through mental, spiritual and physical abuse. They then move on to do the same thing to the next woman. The sad reality is that those men are just as damaged as those women, if not more. They just don't recognize it. I didn't recognize that I was damaged goods either and it began to show in our relationship.

Sexually our relationship was strong, but that began to take a turn for the worse because I wanted sex when I wanted sex. I didn't know how to be romantic, how to cuddle, hold or just kiss. I didn't know how to lay next to a woman without being sexual. Laying next to a woman would get my penis hard and I would be locked into penetrating her and getting mine. Faith did everything in her power to meet my sexual needs by sacrificing her own, which most women do when it comes to men they are involved with.

Faith had become a crutch I leaned on. My life centered on spending all of my free time with her as well as consuming all of hers. During this period, my anti-social behavior began to have an extremely negative impact our relationship. All I wanted to do was sit in the house up under her. When she would invite me out with her, I refused to go because I didn't feel comfortable going out to parties, bars or clubs. Then she would invite me to participate in different family functions, which I would attend, but I would sit there for hours and not talk to anyone. To be honest, I just didn't know how to be social. In my mind, I was being social by minding my own business. I engaged in certain conversations that I related to and would keep my mouth closed if I couldn't relate.

This anti-social behavior that I displayed heavily was a result of how I conditioned myself in prison. In prison, when you are in a large room full of people, your security senses take over. You begin to scope the room for potential danger and even though that danger might not be meant for you, you are always operating as if it is. I built up certain defense mechanisms that would automatically kick in because I trained myself that I couldn't trust my environment and the people who existed in it. This thought process ultimately impacts how a person deals with someone on an interpersonal level, which is very shitty at best.

In prison it is rare to hold a healthy conversation. Prisoners and prison guards often talk with the intent to try and get over on one another and most conversations are centered on exploitive relationships. More bluntly, guys in prison are developing strategies on how to get over on each other every minute of the day. Can you imagine experiencing this type *animalistic behavior* for 5, 10, 20 years or even longer without being negatively impacted in some form or fashion?! Men and women are being released from prison after years of this type of *indoctrination* and are expected to make a successful transition back into society. *Yeah right*!!!

To take this a little deeper, I am 38 years old and have spent over half of my life in some type of incarceration or institution. This has *shaped* how I interact with my family, friends, women, children and society as whole. I wasn't the only person to be deemed special enough to spend over half of their life in prisons, juvenile detentions, precincts, county jails, probation offices and before parole boards as the best option to correct human behavior. Millions of Black, Brown and even white human beings have suffered from this same type of anti-social institutionalization. The reality is that incarceration is not the answer to correcting human behavior and it actually does the opposite by creating worse human beings who become more savage criminals. I have been home from prison 11 years and I still find it difficult to break out of my anti-social behavior. *This is a battle I will continue to fight for the rest of my life…to be a human being in every way possible.*

Eventually I found work through another temp agency. This job was as a garbage man in Inkster, Michigan. One of my partners I had been locked up with put me up on it. The only workers that were guaranteed to work were the drivers and they picked the workers they wanted to go out with them. If you didn't have a cool relationship with one of the drivers more than likely you wouldn't work that day. We had to be there by 5AM and the drivers didn't leave out until 6AM, returning about 6PM.

My partner got cool with a few drivers so, every time we showed up we were selected to go out. We worked four out of five days on 12 hour shifts from 6AM to 6PM and were led to believe that we would get paid for the extra two hours we worked. We were also led to believe that we would make more money for all the extra garbage we loaded on our truck. When Friday rolled around and we picked up our checks, we realized that we were not compensated fairly for all of our hard work. To say that we were disappointed, would be an understatement, but there wasn't shit we could do about it! We had no one to complain to and we didn't have a union that represented us so, we vowed never to work that job again! Even though we needed the job, we refused to allow a paycheck to dictate our self-worth. We also recognized that the adventure of driving through racist white cities such as Dearborn and Dearborn Heights wasn't worth it.

After quitting that job, we got another job working at the airport off of I-94 Expressway. DTW Airport was a huge place and the thought of getting lost in there scared the hell out of me! After working there for a couple of days my nightmare would become a reality. I was running behind cleaning the bathroom and it was close to the time I got off. The person I was working with left me in the bathroom and once I got outside I had no idea which direction to go in. It took everything in my power not to panic. I managed to remain calm and retraced my steps back to the bus we all rode to the airport in. When I got to the bus my partner shouted out, "we wasn't leaving without you bro!" I was excited to hear that.

One of the biggest challenges I faced after leaving prison, was feeling like I had no one I could turn to. In prison I was always able to develop a codependent type of relationship with at least one of the hundreds of prisoners I was encaged with. I could go to that person and borrow a stamp, toothpaste, soap, noodles, etc., and they could do the same with me. I was also able to bare my soul with a person who wouldn't judge me and vice versa. That type of relationship is so important in human development. I know many us have conditioned our minds to believe that we are an Island to ourselves, but that is a *lie* that we have made ourselves believe! We are all codependent on each other in some form or fashion. It is just a matter of developing strong relationships with dependable people that we can rely on in our time of need. We should ask ourselves; out of the hundreds of people we know, how many of them can we count on? That is an important question we should be asking ourselves everyday in our quest to be the best human beings that we can be.

Unfortunately, the job at DTW had been short lived and I wasn't having any luck in finding a new job. It had been several months since I last worked. During this time, Faith enrolled her youngest son in Head Start in Highland Park, Michigan and I would volunteer a couple of days per week in his classroom. From volunteering I learned that Head Start was in the process of introducing a new outreach program called the "Fatherhood Initiative." I attended the first meeting and one after that. I liked what they were talking about in regard to advocating for men and helping them find employment in order to become better fathers.

I enjoyed volunteering in the classroom and interacting with the children and many of them took to me immediately because they enjoyed the company of being with a man/father figure. My mama would often ask me, "Why weren't you using your time to look for a job, because volunteering isn't going to pay the bills?"

Unfortunately, during this time, my relationship with Faith went from bad to worse. A lot of it had to do with me *sabotaging* our relationship with my insecurities and nitpicking about petty shit, coupled with my extreme anti-social behavior. One day she told me that she couldn't tolerate my bullshit anymore and that is was over. I was shook initially, but I eventually got over it and moved on. We remained friends after our break up.

Sometime after our relationship, I started dating an older woman name Tammy. She was brown skinned with short hair and was thick in all the right places. Our relationship was more like a vacation that I desperately needed. She allowed me to stay at her apartment when I wanted to get away to just relax and think. Our relationship was the first relationship that I felt comfortable enough to display my intelligence in and I introduced myself to her as "Yusef" instead of "Joseph". Our conversations covered everything from local issues to world issues and we shared the same passion for making this world a better place.

However, it was in the bedroom that this woman would have the greatest impact on me. One night I climbed into bed with her, got my rocks off and called myself about to go to sleep. She jumped up and yelled, "no you don't think you about to get yours and say fuck mine. It ain't even going down like that nigga!" She had me kiss on her and rub on her as she made herself cum.

Our sexual relationship was more like "Sex 101" for me. She taught me how to be romantic by engaging in *four-play* with her and how to be sensual. She taught me how to perform oral sex on her. She also taught me how to have dirty talk with her while we had sex. One night we were doing it doggy style and she was yelling at me to "do it harder!" I did everything in my power to comply with her demand that I fuck her as hard as I could. This went on for like 20 minutes straight. She was enjoying it so much that she came and squirted all over me. I thought she had urinated on me and I didn't know whether to stop or keep going. That would be my first time experiencing a woman cum like that. Being romantic with a woman was something I had seriously lacked and this older woman was the first woman to demand that I learn to satisfy her needs. In turn she was inspired to please me even more. Unfortunately, men in this country lack that sort of education which has a negative impact on how we view and treat our women in relationships, sexually and otherwise!

I chose to talk about my sexual relationships in order to *educate* young men and men in general that being with a woman is more than just "fucking the shit out of her!" You have to stimulate her mind and spirit, which will ultimately stimulate her body. To a woman, there is nothing more attractive than a God fearing man who is intelligent and demonstrates these qualities in every way possible.

I also chose to *educate* young women and women in general about the importance of demanding that men treat them like a quality woman and not like a hooker they picked up for a good fuck! If the man you are with can't meet the demand that you be treated like a quality woman, then you need to give his ass the boot! Every woman deserves to be treated like a Queen because your essence is that of a Queen. However, you should not be in search of a King to rule you, but for a man/souljah to serve you mentally, spiritually as well as physically.

Teaching the Babies

Chapter 5

My involvement in the Fatherhood Program and my volunteer efforts at Head Start afforded me an opportunity to get a job through their employment program. I was assigned to work as the assistant to the Parent Involvement Coordinator, Ms. Hutchinson. She was a parent who was ultimately hired in at Head Start. Ms. Hutchinson then worked her way up the ranks to hold the job position that was the heart and soul of the Head Start program. Her position directly dealt with the parents of the Head Start children by engaging them through a variety of comprehensive program initiatives which provided them with resources and training on how to become better role models for their children. It was a great honor to be her assistant.

My duties included taking notes at the parent meetings and policy council meetings which discussed the Head Start budget and Head Start program for the year. I was also in charge of calling all parents to remind them of the parent meetings, distributing fliers to classrooms to be passed out to the parents and making sure all of the Parent Involvement files were organized. Since Head Start was a federally funded program, it could be subjected to an audit at any time so the files had to be updated and organized properly.

Head Start is a program which began as part of President Lyndon Johnson's war on poverty. The mission of Head Start is to "promote school readiness by enhancing the social and cognitive development of children through the provision of educational, health, nutritional, social and other services." Head Start is one of the longest running programs still in existence, which was developed to address poverty in amerikkka. Head Start has serviced over 28 million preschool aged children since its inception. It is also responsible for funding the popular television program "Sesame Street" operated by the Carnegie Corporation Preschool Television project which has been instrumental in assisting an innumerable amount of children with reading comprehension, social development, conflict resolution and team building skills, etc.

Head Start and I was a perfect match because it mirrored the Black Panther Party's (BPP) "Free Break Fast Program". The Panthers cooked and served food to Black children in oppressed Black communities because many Black families couldn't afford to feed their children before they went to school each morning. The Free Breakfast Program initiated by the BPP became such a successful program in oppressed Black communities that the Panthers began setting up Free Breakfast Programs across amerikkka in urban cities where they had Black Panther Chapters. It is reported that the BPP Chapters were feeding over thousands of Black children every morning before they went to school. The BPP's Free Breakfast Program was a comprehensive national food service program which met the nutritional needs of impoverished Black people and Black children in particular. In meeting the needs of feeding Black children, the BPP were providing them with a realistic opportunity to reach their full academic potential by starting their school days off on full stomachs. It is difficult for any child to pay attention to their teacher when their stomachs are empty. Currently, there are thousands of children (Black, Brown and white) across this country who attend school every morning on empty stomachs, which has a negative impact on their ability to effectively learn in school.

What the BPP was able to achieve nationally through their Free Breakfast Program had such a powerful impact that the federal government decided to "hi-jack" it and provide a similar program of their own for public schools across the country. The Federal Bureau of Investigation's "FBI" Director J. Edgar Hoover made it his mission to destroy the BPP and in September of 1968 he proclaimed to amerikkka that the BPP was, "the greatest threat to the internal security of the country." Through the FBI's Counter Intelligence Program "COINTELPRO," they used such tactics as discrediting members, planting false reports in local newspapers, forging letters between rival organizations, imprisonment and the outright murder of leaders of the members of different Black, Brown and white radical organizations. The FBI ultimately achieved their goal of disrupting, discrediting and neutralizing the BPP by the wrongful conviction and murder of hundreds of BPP leaders here in amerikkka, all in the name and cause of white justice. When the smoke cleared, the BPP was destroyed and the federal government had stolen their program of feeding children before they went to school.

45

Serving the community through my work at Head Start allowed me to reconnect with what I had become in prison; a servant of the people, a revolutionary! I was inspired to organize my first community youth event so I reached out to my comrad Kwasi who had been home about a year longer than me. The event was titled, "Young Brothas & Sistas on the Move" and it was a huge success. We held the event in the vacant lot next to my mother's house. We engaged young folks in a series of discussions about life. We posed the questions and the youth provided the answers from their young, but real perspectives. This afforded us an opportunity to not only showcase the youth, but to provide them with a voice and offer them support and mentoring as needed. Kwasi and I reached out to our networks and because of their support; we had plenty of food and giveaways for everyone. Our supporters included Wayne County Commissioner Jewel Ware, Wayne Metro Head Start, White's Records and the Moorish Science Temple of America, which donated customized t-shirts with "Young Brothas & Sistas on the Move" emblazoned in red, black and green. Also, a few of the youth and I recited a poem we co-wrote mirroring the title of the event.

Young Brothas & Sistas are on the move,
Young Brothas & Sistas got a point to prove.
That's why we participate in this groove.
We are here today because we ain't no fools,
To get that knowledge we don't get in school.
Society says Young Brothas & Sistas,
Won't make it to a certain age
But we got to stay strong and intelligent,
That is the only way we can prove them wrong.
Sure some Young Brothas & Sistas have failed
But we still represent for them because we all will prevail.
Young Sistas think, so you can maximize your potential & talents,
So you can be successful & move on in life.
We know they try to put you down for being young mothers
But that wasn't a mistake but a lesson to be learned.
Young Brothas being thugs & gangstas will get you burned.
We salute those who died,
struggling to make sanity out of an insane world.
They didn't get a chance to play or pretend,
but they are our special friends.
They were courageous & strong even though they died,

before they were grown.
Those dark & stormy nights are from those people that hated,
But thanks to our Ancestors for showing us the way…
We still made it!
For the Young Brothas & Sistas who have the courage to overstand,
To be creative & not destroy the things in life,
We extend our hands because we are only doing God's work!
We are here to bring BLACK LOVE not BLACK HURT
Because Young Brothas & Sistas are on the MOVE!!!!

This poem was electrifying because it captured the essence of what it meant to be a young Black person growing up in the *'hood*. It *expressed* hopelessness, violence and teen pregnancy as well as the potential for every young Black person to succeed despite being surrounded by the social ills that were seeking to devour them.

These were the first steps I had taken as a community organizer and activist so I was extremely proud of the turnout. Faith brought her children and all of her nieces and nephews and many of the youth from the neighborhood attended as well. We had over 50 youth as well as their parents in attendance. I also took this opportunity to recognize Mother Feebie, a long standing community organizer in my neighborhood who organized free lunch programs every summer for neighborhood children. She also kept one of the abandoned lots cleaned so neighborhood children had a peaceful place to play and enjoy their youth in a community that was surrounded by 'hood hostility and violence. I gave Mother Feebie an award as a token of my appreciation for her undying service to my neighborhood. It was the first time someone had recognized her labor of love and she had been an active community organizer in my neighborhood for over 30 years, doing most of the work by herself.

Mother Feebie was a beautiful woman that loved the neighborhood children with all her heart. Her service to our neighborhood wasn't dependent upon a grant, but was a labor of her love and efforts to secure a future for ghetto youth, with hopes to prevent them from getting mixed up in a life that would ultimately send them to prison or take their lives at an early age. Mother Feebie was determined to make a difference in the community every day until she was found dead in her bed a few years ago. I found a small measure of peace in knowing that I was able to honor her before she left us. Unfortunately, so many of us wait to recognize people after they are gone. I strongly suggest that you give a person their flowers while they are still here, especially if they deserve them!

The type of commitment Mother Feebie displayed to the youth is *missing* in our neighborhoods. Tragically, many of the non-profit programs that are receiving millions of dollars to provide the social programs that most urban communities so desperately lack, aren't providing them. Detroit feels like the capital of non-profits, which create high paying salaries for many folks who are doing poor ass jobs in serving the people they are receiving the money for. Many of these non-profits are actually profiting off the misery of the people they are supposedly serving. As long as the work they do is dependent upon a grant, it will be limited. I am not opposed to grants, but a grant is only as good as the grant writer! More importantly, once the grant money stops coming in, many of these social programs immediately die. Many of the foundations that supply grants have created an atmosphere of severe competition among various non-profits who seek funds from them. However, they failed to support individuals like Mother Feebie with the funding to expand on the great work she was doing in her community. The people suffer immensely because of this *dog-eat-dog mentality* of non-profits. Instead of many of the non-profits working together, they are fighting against each other for the funding as well as crossing each other out!

The days of working in the community as a *labor of love* are slowly but surely coming to an unfortunate end. Once folks began to realize that they could get paid for working in the ghetto, they developed a "fuck working for free" mentality and poverty pimping programs became the calling of the day! I overstand just as much as anyone that funding is a *crucial* element in community organizing. However, once folks begin to solely depend upon foundations and grants, it eliminates the need to demand that the people invest in their own salvation and liberation by reaching into their own pockets. The message here is that we need money, but more importantly, we need your *human capital* to make this work. Our ability to community organize cannot solely depend upon one funding source. We need everyone fully invested in order to improve the quality of our communities and the quality of our people. If folks don't invest in their own communities, then even with grant funding, we all fail.

My temporary job at Head Start was coming to an end and I had no idea what I was going to do next. Luckily, while I was in the office filing one day, Ms. Hutchinson walked in and handed me a job post for an assistant teaching position at Wayne Metro Head Start. Before I could utter a word, she said, "I don't want to hear that you can't be a Head Start Assistant Teacher, because most of the teachers started off just like you did as a volunteer, including myself!" I responded by saying, "that is true, but none of y'all had been to prison either." Her rebuttal was so quick that she cut me off. "I don't want to hear about you being in prison, because over the last two months there hasn't been a more qualified person working with the parents and the children than you!" At that moment I decided to apply for the job. Ms. Hutchinson helped me write my resume and also had a parent do a mock interview with me to prepare me for the actual interview.

Most of the interview was a breeze with the exception of the prison topic. I was nervous but managed to stay cool, because she allowed me to explain my side of the story and didn't judge me based upon my past.

"At the age of 19, I was convicted of assault with the intent to rob unarm, a crime I didn't commit. However, I do recognize that I helped create the atmosphere which led to my conviction because I was guilty of being a member of the gang Zone 8 that committed the crime. Going to prison allowed me to meet my father for the first time and his redemption became the difference maker in my life. This is why I am sitting in front of you as a redeemed and transformed man!" I ended my presentation by admitting that I wasn't an angel and had committed my fair share of crimes in my youth, which I had never been caught for. She sat and absorbed everything I said and responded by saying, "The man sitting in front of me today is a changed man and it would be an honor to have you as a staff member with us!"

I was extremely thrilled after receiving the news that I had been hired. When I left out of her office, I cried tears of joy. Even if I hadn't gotten the job, I was just excited by the fact that she had allowed me to explain who I was. She didn't just judge me by the *yes* I had checked in the box on the application indicating that I had been convicted of a crime.

The question asking whether a person has been convicted of a crime on a job application has provided a rebirth to the old "Jim Crow Practices" by allowing businesses to openly *discriminate* against people who have been convicted of a crime.

The greatest lesson I learned from that experience was the importance of a person's character. Because of the character I had displayed until that point, many of my potential co-workers wrote letters of recommendation on my behalf. However, I believe my choice to be honest in a situation where a lot of people are too afraid to openly admit their past, is what ultimately secured the job. Our character is the most valuable thing we own and we should be working everyday to cultivate that value!

I had been home a little over three years and finally made it off parole. This was a challenge in and of itself. Even though I had not gotten into any trouble, I was living in a high crime infested community which prompted the police to stop me for "driving while Black" and "walking while Black". When a parolee reports to their parole agent, you have to fill out a form that asks whether you have had any contact with the police since you lasted reported. I would always report my contact with the police even though nothing ever came of it. My agent found it hard to believe that the police would just stop me for no reason and I shot back by saying, "that is easy to say that when you are not a Black male!"

However, my parole agent recognized that I had finally secured stable employment and had just organized my first community event, so my future was beginning to look bright. I was also feeling good about myself and had begun to set my eyes on enrolling into college.

Unfortunately, my son wasn't doing so well in school so I enrolled him into a charter school in Highland Park, Michigan. I was feeling good about this decision and believed things were looking up for him until I received a phone call advising me that he was being expelled for having a marijuana "joint". I found out that another student had brought the joint to school and that my son had tricked him out of it so that he could sell it. The school administration's solution was to expel them both even though there was only a little over one month left of school. They didn't want to hear my argument that they should explore preventive and other corrective measures with my son and the other student. They wanted my son off their grounds immediately!

Going through that experience was a flash back for me. It made me reflect on the fact that every school I went to as a young boy had given up on me. Most of the school administrators are so beat up and overworked that they don't have the energy to provide the best quality services for the Black children who are suffering from numerous social problems, which handicap them from excelling in school. Then there are the school administrators that are so out of touch with the social problems that some Black youth are subjected to, that they fail to recognize the need to intervene. Their only solution is to kick them out and move on, continually recycling that process as if it were a concrete solution. When they do this, the message they are sending to the parents and more importantly to the students is that they ain't shit and because they ain't shit, they ain't worth fighting for!

School administrators have to be dedicated to going the extra mile in order to meet many of the social needs of today's youth, especially the Black youth. They must give them a realistic chance at excelling academically and not treat them like throw away children. Every school needs strong violence and substance abuse prevention and intervention programs which would help Black youth deal with many of the social ills that are handicapping them every day in their neighborhoods and at school.

My comrad Greer-Bey drove me to the Downtown Detroit Campus of Wayne Community College to enroll and I was super excited. School came easy to me; I just focused on the prerequisite classes that would be transferable to a 4 year university once I graduated. I really enjoyed attending community college, because it was very diverse and the class sizes were small, so the professors had their finger on the pulse of their classrooms.

My job as an Assistant Head Start Teacher was going well and I was still involved in the Fatherhood Program. I also played an integral role in helping them to develop a men's group called the "Men's

Leadership Council". Our objective was to educate fathers on the importance of being involved in the lives and development of their children. I also contributed to the action plan:

Four-Point Plan:

A) *Purpose: To organize men to take a pro-active approach in the Head Start community, by developing themselves to enhance them as men, fathers and husbands. Having a comprehensive approach on combating the vice of absent fathers in our communities and in our households. The Men's Leadership Council will work diligently to mobilize men to be actively involved in creating an environment that is positive and productive for consistent male and fatherhood involvement.*

B) *Goals: In organizing men, our approach with be goal orientated by making our presences felt in Head Start classrooms. This will have a direct result in making a difference in the lives of Head Start children. We will have realistic goals that will serve as a testimony to our undying commitment of being involved in nurturing healthy children and improving the quality of our communities.*

C) *Aims: A man is strong as he pushes himself, and as weak as he allows himself to be. So, our aims will be rooted in our desires to challenge ourselves to be the best men, fathers and husbands we can be. Only a man can honestly challenge another man to improve himself because that man stands before him as a living testimony of the heights he can reach. In improving ourselves as men, we will become better fathers and better partners/husbands. Also, one of our aims will be to create an environment that is conducive to allowing men and women to address the many problems that stagnant the growth of families. We will educate fathers on the importance of team parenting.*

D) ***Objectives:*** *The first thing the Men's Leadership Council will do as an organized body will be to assess the talents of each member because we believe each member has something special to offer our Head Start community, and then we will ask each member to share his talents in providing healthy male leadership and strong presences of being a man/father with our Head Start children. With all members overstanding their self-worth we feel it will better serve us in maximizing our collective talents (the sum is never greater than the whole) in creating programs that will speak to male and family involvement in the Head Start community, while helping each other eradicating the negative vices that plagues us as men and fathers.*

All of the fathers accepted the "Four-Point Plan" and wanted me to be the President of the Men's Leadership Council. I couldn't accept the position because of my assistant teaching position with Wayne Metro Head Start, but it didn't stop me from staying involved. Soon after, the Fatherhood Outreach position became available and I submitted my resume because I had already been doing the work without the title. Although I recognized that if I were hired for the position, I would be taking a pay cut, I was cool with that because I felt I could do a greater good from that position for the Head Start parents and children. Unfortunately, they eventually hired this G.Q. looking guy for the position. His hire re-enforced what I knew, which was that I was too rough around the edges for them. I didn't fit the look they were searching for, although I could do the work in my sleep and had been doing the work.

Months had gone by and the new Fatherhood Outreach guy had been all talk and little action. I eventually lead a campaign demanding that he do his job by writing a letter outlining what we expected from him as Head Start fathers. It was a *touchy* shit-uation for me since I worked for Wayne Metro Head Start and had put myself in a position to be fired. One day at the end of class, a father picking up his child pulled me to the side and conveyed to me that he and the rest of the fathers had my back 100%! I soon learned that he was General Baker, a legendary Detroit activist.

53

In 1964, he was part of a delegation of Detroiters who went to Cuba and met with Fidel Castro, the President of Cuba and his comrad Ernesto "Che" Guervara, the godfather of "Guerrilla Warfare". Upon returning to Detroit, he began to work for a Dodge Main plant in Hamtramck, Michigan. A year later he would be drafted into the army, but declined his enlistment by refusing to participate in what he considered, an unjust war against the Vietnam people. General Baker and other members at the Dodge Main plant began to lead different "Wildcat Strikes" through the organization they started called Dodge Revolutionary Movement "DRUM". Their goal was to end all discriminatory union and employer policies and practices while empowering Black workers. He was ultimately fired for his organizing and protesting, but continued to fight for justice and equality. He also helped co-found the "League of Revolutionary Black Workers" and the "League of Revolutionaries for a New America". He is still actively involved in demanding justice today and his wife Marian Kramer's activist resume is just as impressive as her husband's. She was once a member of the Black Panther Party and was a member of the League of Revolutionary Black Workers as well and is a member of the "League of Revolutionaries for a New America". She is also the Co-Chair of the "Welfare Rights Organization" with Maureen Taylor, an organization which advocates on behalf of poor people who are getting their lights and gas turned off by Detroit Edison "DTE". Marian Kramer and Maureen Taylor are at the forefront of the fight against present Governor Synder, who is leading the attack to cut thousands of Detroit residents' welfare benefits in 2011. General and Marian immediately took me under their wing and passed on their life lessons as long standing community activists.

The Men's Leadership Council brought in different speakers to present to the fathers before they played basketball in the basketball program we had launched. One of speakers who made a profound impact on us, especially me, was former Highland Park City Council President, Earl Wheeler. In his presentation he talked about his journey all over the world as a man, father and a husband. He closed his presentation by reiterating the importance of being an Afrikan man in a white dominated society and our obligation to not only Afrikan people here in amerikkka, but all over the world! I couldn't wait to introduce myself to him and ask him to become my mentor.

Mr. Wheeler graciously accepted my request and immediately took me up under his wing. He got me involved in another men's organization in Highland Park called the "Highland Park Men's Forum".

The Highland Park Men's Forum was founded in November of 1986 with the purpose of promoting social welfare and benefits to the community through outreach programs such as recreational, educational and counseling for Black youth done exclusively by Black men. They organized an annual banquet where they raised money to give away small scholarships to Black youth in the City of Highland Park. They also organized an annual clothes drive with a local department store that matched them with funds. They provided about 20 youth with $100 each worth of school clothes every year. I joined the organization through Mr. Wheeler's request and worked my way up the ranks to become the Vice-Chair. It was a great honor to participate in both of the community outreach programs organized by the Highland Park Men's Forum.

The Highland Park Men's Forum also sponsored my trip to attend the 10th Anniversary of the "Million Man March" in Washington, DC. On the bus trip, I enjoyed listening to all the elder brothers share their experience in attending the actual Million Man March a decade earlier. They recollected on how Detroit had sent the most Black men to the historical gathering. They also said that it was a once in a lifetime and life changing experience for them to witness over one million Black men standing shoulder to shoulder in harmony and love. They shared their disappointment in the lack of follow-up after the march and the failure to spread that harmony and love by making it a way of life in Black communities across amerikkka. During the drive there I had no clue that I had been sitting next to a brother that had been actively involved in the Black Power Movement in Detroit over 40 years. The brother's name was Cicero Love. He had been a member of the "Republic of New Afrika", a Black organization that was founded in Detroit in March of 1968 at the famous Black owned, "Twenty- Grand Motel" on 14th and Warren. Over 500 Black activists and nationalist from across the country came to the table and 100 different Black activists signed the "New Afrikan Declaration of Independence", which declared the independence of Black people from amerikkka. Robert Williams,

55

who was once the President of the NAACP chapter in Monroe, North Carolina, was elected the President of the Republic of New Afrika. He went into exile in 1961 after organizing armed self-defense among Blacks against the KKK. He was still in exile when he was nominated and accepted the position as President of the Republic of New Afrika. He was also a member of the Black organization, the "Revolutionary Action Movement (RAM)". The Republic of New Afrika's roots were tied to the organization "Malcolm X Society", which was founded in Detroit in 1967 with the purpose of carrying out the mission of Malcolm X. This mission was written out in number 8 of the "New Afrikan Creed." "We must organize upon this land and hold a plebiscite, to tell the world by a vote that we are free and our land independent, and that after the vote, we must stand ready to defend ourselves, establishing the nation beyond contradiction." The organization was also governed by the "New Afrikan Creed" as well as the "New Afrikan Declaration of Independence."

Cicero also went on to tell us about the shootout between the police when they raided the New Bethel Church located on Linwood and Philadelphia in Detroit. He conveyed to us that he was there during the raid. Reverend Clarence Franklin was the pastor of New Bethel Church and is also the father of Aretha Franklin. He allowed the Republic of New Afrika to hold their first annual "Nation Day" gathering at his church, in which over 200 people attended. The Detroit Police raided the meeting with their guns blazing and when the smoke cleared one officer had been killed and another officer was injured. More police were called to the scene and upon arriving, they harassed and arrested over 150 Black people and took them all down to the police headquarters. George Crocket Jr., who was a Recorder's Court Judge, went down to the police headquarters and held a bond hearing for all those who had been arrested. The majority of them were released. He took a stand against the Detroit Police Department's racist behavior which was more than evident during their raid. I was in awe of his story. Not because I didn't know about it, but because I had read about it in prison, and was hearing firsthand accounts by somebody who was there when the shit-uation happened. Once we arrived in Washington, DC, I stuck by Cicero's side soaking up as much history from him as I could. I respected him so much that I walked around like his body guard and

56

was ready to take a bullet for him if need be. When we got back to Detroit, he took me up under his wing and began to mentor me into being the activist that I am today.

I ultimately adopted Mr. Wheeler and his wife as my parents. They have been cornerstones in the Highland Park community for over 40 years and have been married for over 50 years. Their life and love for one another has been sustained by their passion and desire to improve their community by any means necessary. Even as senior citizens, they can be seen on the *frontlines,* in the thick of the fight trying to improve Highland Park. What they have been able to accomplish in one lifetime would take many of us two or three lifetimes to achieve!

My relationship ultimately came to an end with Tammy and I started dating this woman who attended Wayne County Community College with me. She lived by herself and had no children. We hit if off well.

Ms. Hutchinson asked me to attend a meeting with her at the "Detroit Parent Network" (DPN), a new parent organization that was looking to expand into the City of Highland Park. There was a round table of about 20 people, with only two being men. Everyone took turns introducing themselves and sharing their journey as a parent. When it was my turn, I spoke strongly about going to prison and meeting my father and how that relationship changed my life. I also spoke about my return to society and my mission to break the cycle of incarceration in my family. Everyone was speechless after I was done talking. When we broke to eat, a woman walked up to me and introduced herself. "My name is Tonya Allen. It is parents like you that will be the driving force in building powerful parents advocating on behalf of their children." She didn't need to say anymore in order to sell me on why I should join the Detroit Parent Network. Tonya was the *type of leader* that people loved to follow and she worked her magic in helping develop you into a leader in your own right. The more I became involved in the DPN through my volunteerism, the more I stood out. I was ultimately deemed "Parent of the Month" and Tonya did a write up on me in the DPN monthly parent newsletter:

Parent of the Month

Joseph 'Yusef' Ruffin exemplifies a good father. He raises his son, DeAngelo, works at Head Start, is a fulltime student at Wayne County Community College and is a community activist. Yet, he has overcome many hardships to be a good dad. Yusef has broken a trend of incarceration in his family. At 19, Yusef served time in state prison and met his father who is serving 25-60 year term. Unfortunately, Yusef also met him in prison. However, Yusef decided that enough is enough! He vowed to prevent his son from ever spending time in prison. Yusef recognizes that sometimes in our society, we forget that prisoners are members of our community. They are brothers, husbands and fathers. The families who are left behind don't get much support. Yusef is working to change that! The Prison Parenting Program is a new effort to engage and assist families of prisoners. The program connects families to solutions and strategies to overcome the devastating impacts of incarceration while meeting the needs of children who have parents in prison.

This would be the first feature to be written on me in any paper. It felt good to read what Tonya had written about me, which re-enforced that I was traveling down the right road. Tonya ultimately left the DPN as the Director and brought in Joy Calloway who continued to do a great job as the new Director by inspiring the staff and parents. Through the DPN, I was able to take classes on facilitation and ultimately became a Certified Facilitator. Before Tonya left, she hired Derek Blackmon who began organizing a monthly "Men's Rap Session" and he asked me to help him kick it off. Derek became a big brother and father figure to me. The Men's Rap Session became one of the most successful men's groups in the state of Michigan and I was ultimately elected to the Board of Directors of the DPN. Tonya and Joy were instrumental in helping me to develop my voice and the DPN not only helped me to become a better man and father but was instrumental in my becoming the community organizer/activist that I am today.

Like Father Like Son:
The Next Generation

Chapter 6

DeAngelo, it has been a long journey & you have made me a better father/man because of it. I love you dearly and I wish your mother was here today to see her son turn 19. Just know it hurts my heart every time I think about how you had to grow up without your mother since the age of two. The day I learned your mother was murdered, I cursed God and begged him to take my life in place of hers, because you needed her more than you needed me and I still stand by that today son. I couldn't imagine growing up in this world without my mother...

By the age of 14, my son was turning into a little social monster right under my nose. He was mirroring some of my childhood ill-mannered characteristics and had become even more disruptive in school. So, I decided to enroll him into Malcolm X Academy, an Afrikan-centered school in Detroit. Upon enrolling him, I told him he needed to read the "Auto-biography of Malcolm X" and purchased the book for him. While he was sitting on the porch reluctantly reading his book with his mouth poked out, my mama approached him to see why he had this ugly look on his face. After a brief conversation with her, he took his book in the house and was about to go run the streets. I immediately stopped him and asked him why he stopped reading his book. He told me that his grandmother said he could go hang with his friends. Before I could respond, my mama came and took over the conversation, "That boy doesn't need to be reading that book. It is too hot outside for that boy to be sitting on the porch reading and plus that book is too big for him to read!" My mama and I got into a heated argument about my son and she won!

I love my mama dearly and I know in my heart that all she wanted was the best for my son, just as she wanted the best for me. However, she had no idea that she was doing him more damage than good by babying him. She was mentally handicapping him and so was his other grandmother. My mama never graduated from high school and was ultimately raised in a street culture that devalued higher learning. Although she recognized the need for an education, it was a limited one.

My mother's act of undermining me as a father was damaging to the relationship I had with my son, because she did it in his presence. My son recognized that he could manipulate his grandmothers and me, so he would pin us against each other often. When he was pissed off at my mama, he would stay with me, when he was pissed off at me, he would stay with his other grandmother and this vicious cycle would be repeated numerous times. Also, during this period I would learn that my son was on the path to earning his Zone 8 thug stripes! The signs were obvious to me because of how much his actions resembled my own at his age. He thought that he was pulling wool over my eyes, but I saw what was coming a mile away! He was trying to *wear* my Zone 8 shoes.

I did everything in my power to protect my son from the ills of street life. I tried to stay one step ahead of him by being extra hard on him as an attempt to break his developing passion towards becoming a Zone 8 thug. Unfortunately, the harder I was on him, the more negative my impact. I eventually pushed him away and he fell even further into the life I tried so desperately to protect him from. His grandmothers didn't help the shit-uation either. Their lack of support for my efforts allowed him to view me as the "big bad wolf" while they were viewed as his protectors. My son did not recognize me as a parent or an authority figure so; he was disrespectful and disobedient towards me. In his eyes, he received better treatment from his grandmothers because they allowed him to do *whatever* he wanted to do. What he didn't realize at the time was that the freedom he was being afforded could ultimately land him in prison or even worse, if he did not change his attitude and lessen his passion for the streets.

Eventually, our relationship took a turn for the worse. One day I went over to my mama's house to pick my son up and he told me that he wasn't coming home with me. I told him that he had no choice in the matter and to my disbelief; he responded by shouting back, "if I had a gun I would blow your muthafucking brains out!" Before I knew it I was on his ass like white on rice! He ran and grabbed the telephone and said he was about to call the police. I left to clear my head and calm down.

I learned later that he did call the police and that they took him to Henry Ford Hospital. The doctors said that he had a sprained neck so Child Protective Services were notified. They started an investigation regarding what happened and we were assigned a social worker. The social worker turned out to be cool so I was straight up with her. I explained that I had let my anger get the best of me and that I took full responsibility for my actions. A counselor was then assigned to us. In the early sessions it was just the counselor and me, because my son would be a no show and his grandmother wouldn't answer or return the counselor's phone calls.

Those early sessions were good for me because they allowed me to get a lot of things off my chest. In one session I expressed to the counselor that I felt like I had let my son down by failing to make him a priority during the early part of my release from prison. By doing so, I gave him the impression that I cared more about the women I was dating than I did about bonding with him. I also went on to express to her how I felt like my mama and his other grandmother had cut my legs off from up under me as a father.

My son had lost his mama to gun violence at the age of two and I overstood that I could never fill the void that losing his mother had left in his life. I had been depending on his grandmothers for that. What I didn't overstand at that point was that although they both loved me and wanted the best for me, their experiences as parents who had to be both mother and father to their own children, didn't allow them to see me as a viable father. My poor decisions helped to solidify their view of me because the only positive thing that they had experienced from men was their ability to help them procreate. Unfortunately, they would be left to raise those children alone. This is an endemic that is plaguing families across amerikkka. Fathers are *abandoning* their children by leaving the mothers to raise them by themselves and at an inordinate rate.

While my son was staying with his mama's mother we would talk periodically on the phone. He ultimately started attending the counselor sessions, but wouldn't say much during them. I wouldn't force him to talk because I overstood that he was carrying a lot of pain from losing his mama so young and in such a violent way. He also carried the burden of not having his father in his life for the first eight years, during which time he had only met me once. Even though I failed at a lot of my

61

fatherly duties, I never failed to tell him how much I loved him. I expressed my love for him every chance that I got. One of the biggest obstacles between fathers and sons is the father's inability to express tender emotions such as love to their sons, because their fathers failed to express those emotions to them.

During this period, my son really started progressing as a Zone 8 thug. One day he was smoking weed with his friends in his grandmother's basement and my mama went over there to deal with the shit-uation. He refused to come out of the basement and neither one of his grandmothers would go down there to get him. My mama ended up calling me over and I went into the basement and had him and his friends come upstairs. Unfortunately, the only time they would call me was when they needed me to discipline my son. Soon after that shit-uation, I was sitting with his grandmothers discussing my son. They were arguing between themselves about which one of their houses my son should stay at. Even though I was sitting at the table, my son staying with me wasn't part of their argument. Listening to them argue almost broke my heart because I realized at that moment that I wasn't even considered as an option. They didn't view me as his father. To them, I was nothing more than a sperm donor. He ultimately went to live with his mama's mother because she wasn't a disciplinarian like my mother and I.

Staying with her was his passport to run the streets freely while under the influence of wanting to be a Zone 8 thug. Word was getting back to me about some of the thug activities he was engaged in throughout the neighborhood and many people were giving him a pass because of me. He was getting his thug weight up by gang banging, stealing and smoking weed and there wasn't anything I could do, because his grandmother was his legal guardian. It was killing me inside! By age 16 my son was a full fledged Zone 8 thug!

Soon enough, his thug activities would come back to bite my mama right in her ass! He had stolen 1 of 3 brand new flat screen TVs which belonged to my sister's father, right out of my mama's house! Nobody realized it was missing until my sister's father came over and asked where the other TV was. He took the remaining two TVs home. Shortly after that, two young men ran up in my mama's house through her back door and pulled a pistol on her demanding the TVs. Once they realized they weren't there, they left. My mama called me crying and explaining what had just happened. I stopped what I was doing and went to my neighborhood. It didn't take long to find out that my son had stolen the first TV and sold it to one of the homies in the neighborhood. He denied having anything to do with the guys pulling the gun on my mama, but did finally admit to stealing the other TV. Since the street mentality is a parasitic shit-uation where guys in the street life double cross each other as a way of life, it is a strong possibility that his *road dawgs* had double crossed him in order to rob his grandmother. The *streets breed* an "I don't give a fuck" mentality and everybody is a potential prey or victim for those who are trapped by that predator mentality.

My mama, my son and I were in her kitchen trying to get to the bottom of what had happened. We were trying to make sanity out of an insane shit-uation, but during our conversation I was doing all I could do to control my anger. I couldn't believe some guys had run up in my mama's house and pulled a gun on her! However, my son wasn't paying us any attention and then finally blurted out, "Y'all can get on out my face, because I ain't done shit!" Before I knew it, I was all over his ass again! Child Protective Services got involved again and I realized after that incident that the best thing for my son and I was to put some space between us. All the hell and pain I had caused my mama had truly come back to bite me in my ass! The saying, "you reap what you sow" came true in my life!

The space between my son and I allowed us to grow closer and to move beyond the hurt that existed. He was still doing his street thing, but he was open to hearing what I had to convey to him and used it to the best of his ability. I had to accept the fact that I couldn't make my son be what I wanted him to be, but I had to continue to be a guide in his life. When we weren't together, all I could do was put it into God's hands and hope and pray that he would make the right decisions. Allowing your teenagers to make their own mistakes by letting go is a difficult lesson for any parent to learn! My son had to learn that I meant him no harm by being on him the way that I was. He also learned that the more that he did what he was supposed to do, the less I would be on him. That is a difficult lesson for any teenager to learn!

As a formerly incarcerated Black father in amerikkka, I lived with the nightmare everyday that my son could possibly end up in prison.

With each step that my son was taking down the road which led to street life, my nightmares became more like an inevitable reality. *This ate at my soul!*

One day I got a phone call from my son telling me that he thought somebody had laced his weed with something and he was hearing voices in his head. I drove to my mama's house and found out from my sister that he had taken an "E" (ecstasy) pill and then smoked some weed so; I drove him to the hospital. After coming home from the hospital he was still hallucinating so his other grandmother took him to Detroit Receiving Hospital. They wanted to admit him to a hospital that could treat youth that had abused drugs and had suicidal thoughts. They needed my signature to have him admitted because I was his parent so, I signed. When he was there, he would call me everyday asking me to come and get him and I would tell him that I couldn't come get him until the doctors released him. He was allowed one visit per week so, when his visitation day came, I went to see him. He asked me to bring my first book, "The Window 2 My Soul" so he could read it. The visit went well and I conveyed to him that he had to fight through whatever he was going through. He was ultimately released, but had to go back shortly after that. They kept him for another week and prescribed him with some medication. In the beginning he wouldn't take his medication so his grandmother would call me. I would tell him to take it and he would.

My oldest son DeAngelo is 19 years old now and he is doing much better these days. He has enrolled in an adult education class in order to earn his GED and we are mending our relationship as father and son. We see each other and talk on the phone a few times per week, sometimes just to say "I love you". He is transitioning into adulthood and learning what it means to be responsible and I am being supportive every step of the way.

My relationship with my new girlfriend was going good so we decided we wanted to have a baby and get married. Nicole grew up in a two parent household, so she was determined to duplicate what she had seen as a child. During her pregnancy she called me with panic in her voice saying, "I need you to get over here, somebody is trying to kick in my door!" I was at my mama's house when I got the phone call so, I wasn't that far from her apartment. I asked her to calm down and explain to me what was happening as I drove to her apartment. She explained to me that it was her ex-boyfriend that was kicking on her door, because she wouldn't let him in. She had also called her dad and he got there right before I did. When I arrived, I immediately ran up to her apartment to make sure she was safe. When I got up there Nicole's father was standing in the hallway talking to the guy and I walked right by them to check on her. She was sitting on the couch talking to her mama. I spoke with her to make sure she and the baby were cool and then I walked over and saw the damage he had done to her door. If her parents had not arrived when they did, he would have kicked the door in! The thought of him kicking on her door and what he may have done to her had he been successful in kicking it in, pissed me off instantly! So, I walked out into the hallway and started hitting her ex-boyfriend with everything I had, while dragging him hallway across her apartment. Needless to say, we didn't have any more trouble out of him.

I had this serious cough (which I still have to this day), that I just couldn't shake so, I decided to go to the hospital and have some x-rays done on my chest. My son's mother and I were pulling up in front of my mama's house after leaving the hospital and I noticed a guy mean mugging me. By the time I got to the street, I saw out of the corner of my eye that the guy was running towards me. When I got to the sidewalk, he took a swing at me. I ducked his punch and pushed my son's mama towards the porch to get her out of the line of danger. This guy and I had gotten into it shortly after I was released from prison so, I knew things were about to get ugly.

I was going to the corner gas station on Ferry Park and 14th street and he was standing with one of my little homies in front of the door talking. Instead of walking through their conversation and being rude, I said "excuse me", but the guy responded by telling me to "go the fuck around!" I didn't say anything, but I gave him a *look of death*! He then went into action and tried to hit me in the head with a bottle, but I was able to duck his swing. I left and took the food home that I had just bought from P&J's restaurant. When I got back to the gas station, he was gone. A couple days later I was coming out of Joey's liquor store drinking a cooler and the guy approached me trying to tell me that he didn't mean to try and hit me with the bottle. I listened for a second and then hit him in the head with my cooler bottle. After that, he went to some of the homies to find out who I was and they brought us to the table for a sit down. I thought things were cool after that until about a year later when we got into it again at the same gas station. As I was walking in and he was leaving out we bumped into each other. Since he was into the street game he started talking big shit and drew down on me (pulled out his pistol), like I was supposed to be scared. I responded by saying "real gangstas don't talk about it, but be about it!" I left out the gas station and went about my day.

So, on the day I had just come home from the hospital, he must have drunk some *courage juice* (liquor or beer), or was high. After he swung on me, I started back peddling in order to remove the danger from my mama's house, because some of his partners had jumped out of his car and started walking fast towards us. They looked like they were ready to put down a classic beat down! When they got in front of my mama's house, my youngest sister's boyfriend Ronnie came outside on the porch standing every bit of 6'4 and 250 pounds. Then one of the guys shouted that it was going to be a *one-on-one fight*! Once I heard that, I stopped back peddling and immediately rushed the guy with multiple punches. Once he realized he had no chance, he started walking away. I immediately started walking after him and people were grabbing me and trying to stop me, but at that juncture I was madder than a muthafucker about him bringing that drama to my mama's house. I walked past the guys that came with him and cussed them out while following dude the entire way back to his car. When he got to his car, I cussed him out and then spit in his face. After I spit in his face, he reached in his car, pulled out a gun and pointed it at my face! Everything happened so fast! I was like a deer caught in head lights! The guy turned his head and shot twice and a bullet hit me in my foot! There is no doubt in my mind that I should have been shot in my face, but through the grace of God, instead of being shot in my face, I was shot in my foot!

The bullet went straight through my foot and didn't hit any veins. At the hospital, the doctors were preaching to me about how lucky I was and I agreed with them. A few days after coming home from the hospital, the police at the Third Precinct brought me in for questioning. They started off by telling me that my mama told them that I knew who had shot me. I responded by saying "y'all should be interviewing my mama then, not me". Once they realized I wouldn't tell them who shot me, they told me I was good to go. After they released me, I saw the guy who shot me driving down my street. I flagged him down and informed him that the police had brought me in for questioning and that I told them I didn't know who shot me. He responded by asking me if I wanted some money to keep my mouth closed. I responded by telling him "I was just flagging you down so that you wouldn't tell on yourself!" Even though I was still pissed about him shooting me, I reasoned in my mind that I would have shot me too for spitting in his face on top of kicking my ass!

The streets were talking and they were saying that I was out for revenge based upon my reputation as a former gang member. One day I was at work and a tall, slim Black guy approached me and asked if he could speak with me. I would learn that the guy was there to protect his investment, because the guy who had shot me was selling dope for him. By listening to his conversation, I could tell that he had been to prison so; I cut to the chase and got straight to the point. He was under the impression that I was a street guy, but after talking to me, he realized that it was far from the truth. We ended the conversation on a good note and I committed not to fuck up his runner and he committed to keeping his runner under control.

One month after healing from the gunshot wound, I would have another run-in which would end with a violent injury. I was standing in front of my house talking to one of my little homies and he offered to treat me to lunch so, I jumped in his truck. I only had $10 to my name and I was holding on to it for dear life. When I jumped into the truck with my little homie, it fell out of my pocket and I had no idea I had dropped it. When I got back, my son asked me if I had lost some money because he saw my mama's boyfriend pick some up from the area where I was standing. I reached into my pocket and realized that my money was gone. I immediately went into the house and asked my mama to get my money from her boyfriend. She responded by asking how I knew he had my money and I told her that my son had seen him pick it up. She brushed it off like if it was nothing. I knew this was going to be a big issue because my mama's boyfriend and I didn't get along. We were both men living under my mama's roof and our egos did not mesh well. Although we never had words directly, he would often say things to my mama about me and they would get back to me. So, when her boyfriend came home, I asked him if he had found some money out front and he said, "Yes". I told him that it was my money and then went on to ask him if I could get it back. Our conversation escalated into a huge argument with both of us sharing some unfriendly words with each other.

He finally decided to give me my money, but instead of handing it to me, he threw it in my face. My instincts took over and I smacked him! When I pulled back he cut me across my right shoulder blade down to the tip of my chest. By the time the police arrived, he had barricaded himself inside my mama's house, which was lucky for him, because I had grabbed a bat and was hell bent on beating him down! I left and went to the hospital and had to get staples to close up my wound.

It took a couple of months before I got over him cutting me. He was at the neighborhood store standing in the lottery line and when he turned around, I was looking him directly in his eyes! Right then, I decided to let go of the anger and hurt I had towards him and we moved on as human beings, not as enemies.

Both violent incidents made me reflect on the violent environments most of us are surviving in, in urban amerikkka. In urban amerikkka, violence has become the process of *conflict resolution*. Urban neighborhoods function as third world neighborhoods and the people within these third world neighborhoods take all their hurt and anger out on each other. This is a byproduct of the oppression that they suffer from. They internalized their oppression and begin to imitate their oppressors amongst each other. They don't know how to fight against their oppressors so, they fight against each other. *Oppressed people oppress people!* The hopelessness, hurt , pain, confusion, frustration and anger that is displayed in the senseless violence in urban amerikkka, reflects the deterioration of our self-worth as human beings caught up in a state of suspense of being underdeveloped. An underdeveloped person becomes a warmonger in their community and has no rational of what peace is, because their humanity has been damaged. So, they patrol their neighborhoods as damaged human beings.

These warzone neighborhoods, roamed by warmongers have to become peace zone neighborhoods. Many of these warmongers, who are *damaged* human beings, have the potential of being healed through (tough) unconditional love, care, human investment and development. Once we take war out of their hearts and minds and replace it with peace, then they can become peaceful human beings. We have to have peace in our hearts and minds to be able to demonstrate peace in our daily lives. Only then will peace become an option and violence won't remain the primary response to conflicts. This can only happen when we develop a healthy self-worth as a people in our community and exemplify it in our households, neighborhoods, schools, recreational centers and churches. Strong families produce strong communities which produce safe communities.

My son's mama finally went into labor and I left work witness the birth of my son. Watching my son Kobie come into this world was the most beautiful experience I had ever encountered as a human being. This would be the first time I had spent time with a baby, changed a diaper or fed a baby. I cherished the experience as a new father. One night my son's mama decided to go out so, I stayed with him while she went out. For the most part, everything was going fine until he woke up and wouldn't stop crying. I called everybody I knew and asked them what I should do to stop him from crying. I finally figured out that I needed to change his diaper and then we both fell asleep. When I saw my son walk for the first time, I cried like a baby. I was crying tears of joy and tears of pain. The tears of joy were because of what I was experiencing with my youngest son, and the tears of pain were for what I didn't get a chance to experience with my oldest son. Although I wasn't able to do everything right with my first child, I took pride in learning from those experiences and making every attempt to get things right the second time around. I love both of my sons equally and dearly and they inspire me each and every day to fight as hard as I do to make this world a better place for them and their children.

My relationship with my son's mama would eventually come to an end when she found out that I was seeing another woman. However, our personal issues never interfered with us co-parenting our son and I have been actively involved in my youngest son's life since the first day he was born. He stays with me on the weekends and during the summers. At the beginning of this school year when his mother's car was down, he stayed with me and I took him to school every morning and picked him up. He knows my number by heart and he never hesitates to call me. Both of my sons have inspired me to be the community activist that I am today!

Locked in to Succeed

Chapter 7

Working at head start as an Assistant Teacher allowed me to fulfill my calling as a community activist/organizer. I was able to hone my skills through advocating for parents and their children while developing programs which engaged the parents where they were, as well as inspiring them to better themselves as human beings. I was also able to develop enrichment programs and activities for the children.

The first program I organized was the Fatherhood Olympics, where I recruited over 50 fathers to help create different games to engage the children. Some of the games and activities we came up with were, Digging for Pennies, Going Fishing (we actually had real gold fish), Camping With My Dad, Bowling With My Dad and other activities and games which were not only fun for the children, but they fostered a bonding experience between father and child. Also, all of the mothers were given a rose as a token of respect and appreciation for motherhood. The event was a huge success and they continued hosting it as an annual event after I left. It had a profoundly positive impact on the head start fathers and children so, I am proud that they kept it going. When February rolled around, I organized a Black History program where we honored Mr. Wheeler and his wife for their dedication to improving the quality of life in Highland Park. All of the teachers had their students do a Black history presentation as well. The children were not only able to enjoy themselves, but they took pride in putting on such an important event for their parents. I am extremely grateful to my co-workers for their assistance, because I could not have organized such successful events without them. I also had a great relationship with all the teachers, because I valued the fact that they treated working on behalf of the parents and their children as a *labor of love*. They just needed someone to provide them with the space to actualize it outside of the classroom so, that's where I came in.

Head Start is led predominately by women and I was the only male teacher at Wayne Metro Head Start. It took some adjustment by many of my women co-workers, but since I had worked my way up from being a volunteer to an assistant teacher, I was able to earn their respect as a hard worker and more importantly as a man who cared deeply for the children as well. Because of my compassion and dedicated volunteerism, Ms. Hutchinson nominated me for the Michigan Community Action Agency Association's "Volunteer of the Year Award" and I won! It was the first time in my life that I had ever received an award.

During this period, I started dating one of my co-workers. Her name was Ann and she was in the process of divorcing her husband. She had been in an abusive relationship for over ten years and had four children; three girls and one boy. After her divorce, we got serious and we moved in together, but her children had a hard time accepting our relationship early on. Some days they liked me, other days they couldn't stand me. The way their father viewed me heavily influenced how they interacted with me. Because he had not accepted my relationship with his ex-wife, he fostered a hostile shit-uation between his children and I, which made them standoffish towards me. One day he came over to pick them up and I went outside and greeted him. He looked at me with a nasty look and didn't say anything in response. I brushed off his dirty looks and his lack of response as immaturity and insecurity and I went back inside. As long he didn't say anything openly and out of the way to me, we had no issue. We were living in a two family flat and her sister-in-law lived downstairs from us. She was married to Ann's ex-husband's brother who was incarcerated. One day Ann's ex-husband was over her house hanging in her backyard with her new boyfriend drinking, smoking weed and talking badly about me. Ann's youngest daughter observed their conversation and came and told me that they were bad mouthing me. I went into the backyard and told both of them to "let my name taste like shit in your mouths!"

Ann and I had to overcome some serious personal challenges as we progressed in our relationship, both individually and as a team. Our biggest challenge centered on my relationship with her children. Ann was trying to figure out how to start her life over while living with the pain of being abused mentally, physically and emotionally and while trying to keep the concerns of both myself and her children at the forefront. She was trying to learn to love herself all over again and at the same time learn how to let a man love her. Many women find themselves trapped in abusive relationships, because they have allowed their world

71

to center around a man who has serious self-esteem issues which turn him into a *control freak*. He begins to complain that all of her female friends and family members are in their business too much and out of her love for him and her desire to prove her love, she cuts off all her female friends and distances herself from her family members to prove her loyalty to him. The abuse begins to escalate, because there isn't anybody she can turn to for help as she has cut off her support system. During this process, the woman's self-worth begins to evaporate and she feels trapped on an island of abuse, filled with shame and self-degradation for cutting off her friends and distancing herself from her family. She feels empty inside, because she has no one to turn to. She wants to leave, but if there are children involved, she stays to endure the abuse in order to protect her children from exposure to the outside shame they may be subjected to by family members and friends. The best thing any of us can do to support a person who is in an abusive relationship, is not to judge them and to love them unconditionally. The unfortunate reality is that if many of these women do not seek help for the abuse, someone may end up dying in the relationship, typically the women, if not both due to murder/suicide.

Her esteem,
Can be measured by the height of her stilettos
Easily broken with each crack in her concrete
She walks no taller than they allow
Somebody's neglected child, abused wife, no therapy
Her buried burdens surface across the backsides of her children
Because they can never be enough to ease history's pains
And she can't help but to love the Lord in vain
Because vanity is her only stronghold
Bold and beautiful
Yet her exterior can only carry her so far
She travels through life like a tourist
Uncomfortable in her own home
Inside her own skin
Tormented by the demons within her own psyche
She's running from herself
Working her fingers to the bone for wealth
She'll never find pleasure in having
Stress and waking up are synonyms
And she hates kissing him

72

But marital obligation says that she must
One sided lust,
Is the sum of a union she's already mentally divorced from
She feels like a coward, afraid to leave him for happiness
So she hangs on for convenience sake
Plus the Bible says that she should stay until one of them dies
But she wonders if GOD forgot to include what to do
When you're already a corpse inside
Where do broken hearts and crumbled souls go
Cause she'd rather not go home
But worries about the kids
Convincing herself that he will never hit them
Plus they'll be grown in a few years
So she'll just stick it out
And since flowers occupied his fists when he arrived home
And she doesn't want to be alone
She stays
But happiness lasts only days between punches
Two kicks in between lunch and dinner
Only this time, she's fed up
So she loads clip
Hands him cup
He takes sip
Gun goes click
He drops cup
She drops gun
But she won't run
Cause his last inhale
Is her first exhale
She feels free now
And yeah,
Her esteem,
It still doesn't measure past the height of her stilettos
But for her
It's the first time she can stand tall enough to breathe

"Honeycomb"

My relationship with Ann's children was going from hot to cold
and vice versa, every other day. However, I had reasoned in my mind

73

that I could not love Ann without loving her children, no matter how much the shit-uation was getting on my nerves. At the heart of the problem between her children and I, was that they didn't know how to accept me without feeling as though they were rejecting their father and I had difficulty figuring out how to step into a role where I wasn't welcomed. Although I made every attempt to treat them as my own children, for a period, we were all walking on eggshells! This hectic environment between her children and I, had Ann caught in the middle, because if she showed me too much affection they felt betrayed and if she wasn't as hard on them as I expected, I felt betrayed. I recognize now how much stress this must have caused Ann in an environment that was supposed to be her safe haven after a decade of abuse at the hands of her ex-husband. I commend her for enduring such a challenging time. Also, the person that I have become as an author, speaker, business owner and community activist/organizer/leader wouldn't have been possible without her love and support. It is true that behind every successful and strong man is a successful and strong woman.

Many amerikkkan households across the country are made up of "patch work families", meaning they are missing either the birth mother or the birth father. One of the parents has moved on with their lives and started dating or even married another man or woman. Unfortunately many of the adults treat the children like a *disease,* because they did not conceive them. Or, many of the children treat the adults like a *disease,* because they are not their birth parents. Negligently, adults contribute to this *social nightmare,* because they are influenced by the amerikkkan culture of identifying the children as "step-children" and the children respond by treating and identifying the adults as "step-parents". The term "step" is *counterproductive,* because it does not foster *family-hood.* It draws a strong distinction between a birth child/parent and one who is a sometimes unwelcomed *addition* to what is considered the *real* family.

When I would be out with Ann's children and people would inquire as to whether I was their father while complimenting their manners and beauty, I would immediately respond by saying "Yes!" I would then notice the positive looks in their eyes when I said that and it made me feel great as a man who desperately wanted to be accepted by them as a paternal figure. One day while I was driving with Ann's second oldest daughter, I conveyed to her that if I had a daughter, I would want her to be just like her. In hindsight, I recognize that this was an important bonding moment between us, because I was able to step beyond our personal challenges and recognize and convey my fatherly admiration for her as a positive young lady.

After living with Ann for over 6 years, I realized the trust she had actually invested in me with regard to her children, especially her daughters. There is an *ugly duckling* of fathers, brothers, uncles and boyfriends creeping into the bedrooms of little Black girls, brutally forcing themselves onto them, snatching away their purity and scaring them for life by molesting or raping them. This endemic of molesting and raping girls by savage men has been going on in the Black community for decades, but out of shame and denial, people remain silent and continue to sacrifice precious girls. Many Black people think that this is a white social behavior, but the harsh reality is that this has become a human *social disorder* of innocent young girls being violated by the very men that their safety and trust was bestowed upon!

During this period, through my comrad Kwasi, I joined the organization Helping Our Prisoners Elevate "HOPE", which was founded a year before I came home from prison by school teachers, parents, community activists, prisoner advocates and former prisoners. HOPE was/is a proactive community based outreach organization. Their focus is to aid in the transformation of incarcerated men and women and to build a bridge for these men and women to walk across upon their release from prison. HOPE believes it can contribute towards the transformation of incarcerated men and women by distributing books and other literature to them as a means of potentially raising the informational awareness of those imprisoned. HOPE also made a strong effort towards bridging the gap that separates those who are imprisoned from their family members who remain in the community.

Initially, HOPE sent books directly to those prisoners who requested them or through the family members who requested them. HOPE successfully sent several hundred books to individual prisoners across the state of Michigan. We also donated books to prison libraries. These books varied in content, but most were Black literature, because we wanted to be sure that we would have a positive impact on the prisoners by providing them with an education of their history. We believed if we could change the way a prisoner thought, then they would have a realistic chance in making a successful transition back into society. Malcolm X was our model. He used books as a means to transform his life while he was in prison. We also had members who were living testimonies of that model. Our primary focus in embracing the model of Malcolm X was to reduce the rate of recidivism in the Black community, meaning Black men and women returning back to prison, which was a high probability.

Malcolm X made all the sense in the world, because he epitomized what transformation and redemption was. When you examine Malcolm X's life, you overstand that he was a product of a broken family and a broken community, which produced a broken human being, surviving through broken dreams and underdeveloped and criminal behavior. So, when Manning Marable wrote his book, "Malcolm X: A Life of Reinvention", he did a disservice to not only the legacy of Malcolm X, but to millions of Black families who are still suffering from the social ills that created "Detroit Red", a drug user, pusher, womanizer, petty criminal and worthless human being that had to be incarcerated. Those who incarcerated Malcolm X did not have a goal to cultivate a redeemed human being!

Malcolm X means different things to a lot of different people and the topic of his life has become center stage for conversations across this country, because of the release of Marable's new book. The most important subject that is missing in many of these conversations taking place across the country as they reevaluate the life of Malcolm X is the *foul social* conditions that gave birth to "Detroit Red" in the first place. They fail to acknowledge and address the institutional and open racism that destroyed his family and ultimately contributed to his criminal behavior. Unfortunately, these *foul social* conditions exist today and have given birth to millions of "Detroit Reds" in urban amerikkka. I have stated publicly many times, that I wonder how my life would have turned out if I had read the Autobiography of Malcolm X in my youth. I don't believe I would have become the next Malcolm X, but I am pretty certain that I would not have traveled the path to being a gang member and ultimately a criminal. By default, I became "Detroit Red" with the rest of the young men in my neighborhood that grew up in households that were plagued by absentee fathers. We determined our manhood based upon our street credibility, because our mothers were left with the double duty of being a mother and father, raising us in socially decaying circumstances and with limited resources. They were dying inside from watching their sons become social monsters and renegades, committing social suicide by either imprisonment or an early death.

In the 21st century, amerikkka leads the world in incarceration with over 2.5 million people in prison, half of which are Black. What is alarming about these numbers is that Black people still only make up 14% of amerikkka's total population. The majority of Black men enter prison as a result of growing up in broken homes and in broken neighborhoods and are surviving through broken dreams, which produce broken human beings. These broken human beings see criminal behavior as their only means of survival in their hellish reality. These Black men who find themselves in prison have left their sons to be raised in the same "brokenness" that they grew up in and become empty and heartless like their fathers. Some meet up with their fathers in the streets or in prisons and are ready to devour their fathers, whom they despise.

Black males who grow up in urban environments in amerikkka know more Black males that are in prison than they know in college, which is why they accept their fate of going to prison with such ease. Some embrace it as an *urban rites of passage* or an opportunity to reunite with the homies that they haven't seen in years. To take this even deeper, people who are outside of the Black community fail to overstand that Black males are exposed to drug dealers more than they are exposed to lawyers, judges or doctors as a profession. This is a major contributing factor as to why Black males make up 50% of the prison population here in amerikkka. Mass incarceration in amerikkka has lead to the stagnation and often demise of Black and Brown communities, through the genocide of Black and Brown families and at the expense of Black and Brown youth.

In prison, many Black men have taken the initiative to transform and redeem themselves from being "broken men" into productive human beings as Malcolm X did. They leave prison with the purpose of returning back into their communities as protectors and providers, instead of returning as underdeveloped predators preying on their communities through criminal behavior. This is a result of them using their prison time as an opportunity to begin to go within themselves to heal themselves of the pain and hurt that plagued them to be hurtful human beings, because as the saying goes, "hurt people, hurt people".

77

On more than one occasion, I have been asked by young Black males, "Why do Black men have to go to prison to change their lives?" This is a topic of conversation that we should be conducting as we evaluate the life of Malcolm X, because it is through his life, that we are able to find the answer to that question. We can begin the process of raising healthy Black youth, in healthy Black households and communities, by producing healthy human beings armed with knowledge of self. We can also begin by encouraging them to be committed to being a healthy and contributory member of their community.

Through Malcolm X's life, we are confronted with the reality of children growing up in households without their fathers, mothers being overwhelmed with raising children by themselves and children being co-parented by the streets. This *social nightmare* is a common theme in the lives of notable Black and Brown men, who have survived to tell and write their stories: "Manchild in the Promise Land" written by Claude Brown, "Convicted in the Womb" written by Carl Upchurch, "Makes Me Wanna Hollar" written by Nathan McCall, "Monster: The Autobiography of an L.A. Gang Member" written by Sanyika Shakur, "Always Running" written by Luis Rodriquez, "The Window 2 My Soul: My Transformation from a Zone 8 Thug to a Father & Freedom Fighter" written by Yusef Bunchy Shakur and many other books written by surviving souls of pain, neglect, abuse, mis-education, confusion, abandonment, anger and incarceration. Each story tells the same ugly truth of growing up in urban amerikkka in a subculture of third world conditions, which are manufacturing genocidal soldiers who are hell bent on destroying their communities and themselves. In the process, they find themselves incarcerated as the government's solution to correcting human behavior. When actuality, the real solution is to redefine Black and Brown families by creating healthy households/environments, which will in turn produce healthier Black and Brown men, determined to live out healthier lives.

The Michigan Department of Corruptions/Corrections (MDOC) began to reject the books we were distributing to prisoners. Despite the fact that we were having a positive impact on prisoners who were beginning to take steps in transforming their lives, they based their rejection of the books on HOPE not being recognized as an approved vendor with the MDOC. Instead of giving up the fight of serving the prison population and their family members, we decided to reinvent ourselves through other community initiatives. So, we sponsored bus trips for family members to visit their loved ones throughout the State of Michigan. Our goal was not to make a profit, but to meet a need in our community. Many family members who took our bus trips, had not seen their loved ones for up to ten years and in some cases it would be the first time a child would be seeing the father. We were reconnecting families and reuniting children with their incarcerated parents.

We also published a quarterly community newspaper to promote the work we did as an organization and to educate the community about the importance of getting involved in addressing mass incarceration. We ultimately published a "Re-Entry Manual" for those prisoners who were on their way home after earning parole. It provided them with comprehensive knowledge of what to expect upon their arrival and what programs offered realistic help.

Through HOPE and the DPN, I launched a "10 week Prison Parenting Program" for children who had an incarcerated parent. The program's primary focus was to help children write their incarcerated parents, encourage parents or guardians to involve their child in their incarcerated parent's lives and to help children identify and overcome possible feelings of hurt, sadness, shame and anger due to having an incarcerated parent. From there I organized a community event entitled, "Prisoner Awareness Day", where we gave away school supplies on behalf of incarcerated parents to their children, held letter writing campaigns where children sent letters to their parents and hosted informational workshops around the issues of incarceration. The event was a huge success. Because of the outstanding work we were doing as an organization in the community, HOPE was awarded a grant for $25,000 from Wayne County.

Although I gave many of the members of HOPE pure hell, I give HOPE credit for assisting in my development as the leader I am today. I was like a big burst of raw energy that was ready to explode on the world and that did not make it easy for some of my co-members. However, I learned a lot from them and ultimately worked my way up to the rank of Chair. HOPE has been a sponsor for the annual back to school supply drive, which I have been doing for the last four years consecutively, six times in total. This year (2011), I was able to donate more than 500 backpacks and school supplies to inner city youth, as well as provide food and live entertainment. I am extremely proud of this annual event.

Ms. Hutchinson's informed me about a part-time Fatherhood Outreach position that was open at the YWCA in Inkster, Michigan. I interviewed for the job and was hired on the spot by Karen Gotshaw (RIP). I am grateful that she also didn't allow my past of going to prison to prevent her from hiring me. I worked 20 hours a week and my immediate supervisor Ms. Dunn had just been hired as the Parent Involvement Coordinator. Since the YWCA allowed me to create my own schedule, I was still able to work at Wayne Metro Head Start as an Assistant Teacher and attend Wayne County Community College. Unfortunately, up to that point, the YWCA had a poor history in being able to get fathers involved in the program. So, I partnered with John Fort who worked at Wayne County Head Start, which was over all of the head start delegations in Wayne County. Through my partnership with John, I was able to co-facilitate workshops for parents and staff and he took me up under his wing and schooled me on how to be efficient and effective as the Fatherhood Outreach worker.

In the beginning, I thought my job was going to be a piece of cake, but I would learn that the reason that they had a poor reputation of getting fathers involved was because the YWCA administration never got behind the Fatherhood Program. When I called my first meeting, I had close to 25 fathers come out. I was brutally honest and told them, "I was given a raft to serve you with, but I need a boat. If anybody falls off, it's not my fault!" The fathers respected my realness and liked how I made something out of nothing on their behalf. I had a budget of $1,000 to cover over six Head Start sites in cities such as Redford, Dearborn, Inkster and Garden City. The head start population they covered was one of the most diverse in the State of Michigan, with Blacks in Inkster, whites in Garden City, Arabs in Dearborn and in Redford you had all three. I was determined to succeed despite the odds that were stacked against me. I outlined a fatherhood agenda that would carry us to the end of the school year and presented it to my supervisor. My fatherhood agenda was outlined as such:

1. *Fatherhood T-shirts: The t-shirts will be used as incentives to get fathers involved and a tool to organize*

them around. The t-shirts will say "Fatherhood By Any Means Necessary."

2. *Fatherhood Newsletter: It will be a tool to inform fathers of upcoming events, job opportunities and any other fatherhood related news.*
3. *Male Buddy Days: We would hold Male Buddy days quarterly with different themes. The only expense would be to buy light refreshments.*
4. *Dads Rap Session: Since most men don't like to attend parent meetings, we will hold rap sessions once a month that will be a safe free environment for fathers to engage in honest and healthy dialogue around men issues.*
5. *Male Expo: We would invite a wide range of organizations that offer different services to come out to meet and greet with our fathers and inform them of the services that they offer.*

After I presented my fatherhood agenda, I went to work. Since I knew I was working with my hands tied behind my back and with limited funds, I busted my ass off to serve my fathers. I reached out to different people I had met over the years and built solid relationships with, and asked them for favors. I was able to get a good price on some Black and grey t-shirts, which were a big hit with all the fathers. My supervisors were apprehensive about the message "Fatherhood By Any Means Necessary", because they thought it was a militant message, but I expressed to them that fatherhood was of extreme importance and the message made that point. Our shirts were such a huge hit, that the Fatherhood Outreach Worker at Wayne Metro Head Start had his shirts done with our logo, because we used the same t-shirt printer. He said it was an accident, *Yeah right!* Joy Calloway of the DPN and Allen Martin of "Al Martin Training Services", both came in and conducted workshops for free. They were both a huge hit with the parents. By the end of the school year, I would learn that all of my hard work had paid off, because I was able to improve the fatherhood participation by 90%. It was the first time they had ever had that type of involvement from the fathers.

Being a head start Assistant Teacher re-enforced for me the importance of a father's involvement in the lives of their young children. Children's minds are so impressionable and they gravitate toward men for acceptance and love. The impact this sort of impressionable behavior has on children can either be positive or negative, depending on the type of men who are in their lives. One day we were in class and two of my male students were rapping about being pimps. I immediately told them to come here and asked them if they knew what a pimp was. They said, "No". I explained to them that a pimp dogs women and beats them up. I also inquired as to whether they would want a man to do that to their mothers. Their eyes got big and they both shouted, "No!" I also had a girl student whose mother was late virtually every day to pick her up, because she had to pick up her other child. I would take my student out into the hallway and sing different songs with her in order to ease her fears about being the last student who was picked up. I never complained about the parent being late, because I overstood that she had no one else she could depend on to help her pick up her children. I was committed to not only serving my students but also their parents as well. I took a holistic approach to my making a difference.

During this time, all the children would come to school rapping the song "White-T" by the rap group "Dem Franchize Boys", which was getting major radio play. It wasn't a song that was appropriate for four and five year olds to rap, but instead of chastising them about it, I decided to write a song they could rap in school and at home. The rap went as such:

I come to school, in my white tee. I go by the rules, in my white tee. I brush my teeth until they are white, in my white tee. I sit and write, in my white tee. I say my ABC's, in my white tee. I write my 123's, in my white tee. I play basketball, in my white tee. I don't run the hall, in my white tee. I do positive things in my white tee. That is why I sing in my white tee.

Fundamentally, when you examine Hip Hop/Rap and its impact on our community and youth in particular, you cannot draw the conclusion that it is not negative. Some of the biggest names in Hip Hop/Rap have publicly said that they record two rap albums, one for the general public to listen to and another one for their children to listen to. If their own children don't listen to their general public album, what makes our children less important? Unfortunately, many of us as parents expose our children to Hip Hop/ Rap music by buying it for them, playing it for them while driving them in the car or allowing them to watch MTV or BET (which should be called White Entertainment Television, because it is not Black owned) all day without any filter system. I overstand that many of these artists see Hip Hop/Rap as a way to feed themselves and their families, but they fail to recognize they do it as a detriment to our communities and even themselves. I also overstand that Hip Hop/Rap is a strong reflection of the foul social, cultural and educational conditions of Black amerikkka. If we want to change the state of Hip Hop/Rap, then we have to change the state of Black amerikkka, which heavily influences the lyrics that fuel Hip Hop/Rap. When James Brown recorded his hit song, "I'm Black & I'm Proud", it wasn't like he just woke up one morning and decided to go into the recording studio and record that song. He was heavily influenced by the Civil Rights and Black Power Movement, as well as numerous other artists who were inspired during that time to record songs which contributed to a sense of social pride and responsibility amongst our people. We need to develop that same type of movement here in the 21st century to impact and influence artists of today to contribute to music, what James Brown and other artists of his time once did. We have to overstand as well, that Hip Hop/Rap artists are nothing but pawns in this musical game of menticide (A systematic destruction of a group's minds with the ultimate objective being the extirpation of the group. Bobby Wright), because it's white music executives that are sitting in the back ground controlling and manipulating the careers of all successful Hip Hop/Rap artists. They are feeding our communities with poison via radio air waves, while they are collecting millions of dollars off of our genocide.

I would eventually leave Wayne Metro Head Start to work solely for YWCA Head Start, because I felt like I had maxed myself out there. It would end up being the best decision for both parties, as they benefited from what I brought to the table and I benefited from the experience I was able to gain there. With that experience, I would eventually apply for and be hired as, a Teacher with Southeast Head Start in Detroit. This brought me great pride, because I was able to bring my experience, talents and passion back to Detroiters with an undeniable commitment to making a difference. I couldn't have found two better environments to work in than Wayne Metro Head Start and YWCA. They provided me with the platform I needed to become the community activist and organizer that I am today. They also gave me the breaks that I needed to build up my confidence in organizing and advocating, and provided me with the space to actualize and hone my talents as an activist. Detroit Head Start became my destination to live out my mission of making this world a better place as a *revolutionary*.

Writing & Speaking From the Heart

Chapter 8

I was assigned to work at Southeast Head Start's Male Academy. It was the only Head Start site in the State of Michigan that serviced all male students. What also made this site unique was the fact that the entire staff was male too. The Male Academy was meeting the needs of promoting positive Black male role models in the City of Detroit where households are headed by single Black mothers at the rate of 80%. Through this initiative, we were able to give young Black males a daily and healthy dose of positive and productive Black male images, which helped to shape how they saw themselves in a productive way.

I took pride in my job. I overstood the importance of having a productive and positive man in a child's life, because I lacked that in my own childhood. Because of the impact that the streets had on my views of what men were supposed to be, I strived to do my part in preventing the children in the Male Academy from mirroring my fate. My own experiences afforded me the ability to recognize that many of my students had social issues that were handicapping them academically. I was able to relate to them not only as their big brother, but as a teacher and more importantly, as a father figure. Eighty percent of the boys that were in my class had fathers who were *missing in action* and they lacked positive male role models. For the most part, 90% of their interaction was with women. Many of my students called me dad because for the eight hours per day that they were with me, they were my sons. Most of them could not wait to come to school and be with "Mr. Joe." I encouraged them all to call me that, because I felt that it was a more appropriate and personal greeting.

My students were fascinated with superhero characters so, during story time many of them would take turns telling their favorite Spiderman, Batman or Superman stories. One day when they were arguing about who would tell their superhero story first, I jumped into the argument and said, "I want to tell the story of the Blackman." They all stopped arguing, looked at each other and then looked at me and asked, "Who is the Blackman Mr. Joe?" I told them that the Blackman road an elephant over mountains fighting evil men and his name was

Hannibal the Great. I told them that there was another Blackman named *Chaka Zulu* who fought evil invaders who were trying to capture his family. I also told them about the many Black men who are lawyers, policemen, doctors, firemen, garbage men and mailmen who are doing amazing things every day in our community. They all enjoyed my story so; during story time they would ask me to tell them another story of the Blackman. Soon, many of them began to say that they were the Blackman!

In February of 2006, a reporter from the Detroit Free Press came in to do a story on the Male Academy. One of my students jumped at the opportunity to recite a poem that we were learning to the reporter. "I'm unique! I come from Kings and Queens. When you look at me, what do you see? I'm proud to be me!" Then all the students started reciting the poem. I was a proud teacher that day. I never hesitated to teach them about our glorious Afrikan history and they were always receptive to learning it.

In the summer months, Head Start Teachers are laid off and collect unemployment until it's time to go back to work in the fall. So, I picked up a part-time mentoring job at Kabaz Cultural Center located on the eastside of Detroit, for their summer youth program. The Director of the program was Mama Ayo. For over 30 years every summer as well as in the fall, their doors were open to the youth providing classes in chess, drama, Afrikan dance, computers, basketball and Afrikan drumming. What made her program so special in the summer of 2006 was that a few of the instructors were men who had been to prison and all of us represented redeemed human beings. Mama Ayo believed that men who had overcome incredible odds were in a good position to teach Black youth who were facing many of those same challenges that we had succumb to. She also recognized that we represented a model of how to overcome those challenges. We provided them with invaluable knowledge through our personal experiences, life lessons and preventive measures for avoiding the path to social suicide.

I enjoyed working closely with a brother named Ali Morgan-Bey who was from Highland Park, Michigan. He was a real brother who was committed to making a difference, but was catching hell trying to make a successful transition back into society like so many others. I was also excited to learn that my comrad Seven the General would be performing at the end of our summer celebration. The students loved his realness and rawness, because it captured their young minds. I met "7" in prison and I was the first guy to take him up under my wing and school him on how to do his time wisely. I also gave him books to read. When he saw me, he ran up and gave me a big hug. It was our first time seeing each other since we were in prison and neither one of us knew that the other one was home. He thanked me for taking him up under my wing and gave me the news that he was signed to the independent Hip Hop/Rap label "Legendz Entertainment". He was also working on his solo album, "Bout Time". Since that day, Seven the General has become a rising star in Detroit and has written for and performed with major artists such as K'jon (On Everything ft. Seven the General), D12 (Bizarre & Kuniva), along with Royce da 5'9 & Redman (Rap's Finest-Bizarre of D12 ft. Kuniva D12, Seven the General, Royce da 5'9 & Redman).

While in prison, I knew I wanted to write a book about my life. However, I didn't write it while incarcerated because I was too much in the thick of the fight at the time. I overstood the importance of books first hand, because it was books that took me off my death bed and resurrected me through new information. The knowledge I obtained through books helped to shape me into the man I am today by allowing me to go inside myself and heal myself of the pain and hurt that had handicapped me as human being who was caught up in the suspense of being underdeveloped. One day at a community event I met Essence's bestselling author Michelle Moore from Detroit. I introduced myself to her and shared my aspirations for writing a book. She didn't hesitate to tell me everything that I needed to know. Also, during this time, my comrad Shaka who was still incarcerated, had written and started working on publishing his first book "Crack", a street novel, so he encouraged me to write my book as well and provided me with information of self-publishing. I ran into Michelle again at another community event some time later and she asked me how my book was coming along. I responded by telling her that I was still working on it in my mind. She conveyed to me that it wasn't doing me any good to write the book in my mind and not on paper. What she said struck a nerve inside of me and I decided that day that I would dedicate myself to writing it. I temporarily stopped being active in different community organizations and events and focused all of my energy on writing my book and graduating from college.

I would eventually graduate from Wayne County Community College with an overall 3.22 GPA in Liberal Arts. I was super excited about graduating and I immediately went to my neighborhood and shard the news with all my homies. I would become the first person from our neighborhood with my type of background to go to college and graduate. What made this accomplishment mean so much to my neighborhood was that Northwestern High school was located right in the heart of our neighborhood, but over the last 30 years, only about ten guys from my neighborhood had graduated with their high school diplomas. It was the proudest moment in my life to have my mama watch me walk across the stage in my cap and gown to receive my college degree. It was the first time I had graduated from anything.

At work, everything was going well although they moved the Male Academy into a new building. I was still determined to take my teaching to another level with a new group of Black boys and all of my new students took to me. One day during class, I was listening to Bob Marley's song "Buffalo Soldier" and my students started singing the song. I begin to incorporate the song into our daily class time so, whenever I shouted Buffalo Soldiers, they would stop what they were doing and lineup. They took pride in being called Buffalo Soldiers. During this period, I wrote a chant for us to recite when we would walk through the hallway. The name of the chant was "Mighty Mighty Boys" and it went as such:

One, two, three, four, we are the Mighty Mighty Boys of the Male Academy knocking at your door. Five, six, seven, eight, through Southeast Head Start we are going to be great. Nine, ten, we are beautiful Black boy's growing to be beautiful Black men. Eleven, twelve, we are learning how to be good Black males!

Their parents loved watching their sons march through the hallway disciplined and reciting our chant. It was a beautiful sight to see. I was doing such a good job with my students that my supervisor decided to switch a boy named Nigel into my class because he was giving the women teacher's pure hell. They wanted to write Nigel off as a boy who needed medication. However, Nigel was super smart, but had a few behavioral problems and always wanted his way. Once he realized that he wasn't about to get his way with me after watching his classmates have fun while he was in time out, he started to correct himself. When he would start acting up, I would get his attention by asking him, "Nigel you are too smart to act what?" and he would respond by saying "Dumb Mr. Joe." There is no such thing as a bad child. They are just active as hell and we have to channel their energy positively. When we don't do that, their behavior becomes negative. I had Nigel work with me as my little assistant because I overstood most of my students learned better from their peers and Nigel took pride in teaching his peers what he knew.

When we would be in the gym, my boys would be fighting and arguing over the basketballs so one day I shouted, "Brothers don't fight Brothers!" "Brothers love Brothers!" That day we established "Brother-Law" and "Brother-Love".

Brother-Law

1. *Brothers don't fight brothers.*
2. *Brothers don't spit on brothers.*
3. *Brothers don't take balls from brothers.*
4. *Brothers don't run in the hallway.*
5. *Brothers don't tear up books.*
6. *Brothers don't kick brothers.*
7. *Brothers don't scream in the classroom.*
8. *Brothers don't steal from other brothers.*
9. *Brothers don't talk back to their teachers.*
10. *Brothers don't hit girls.*

Brother-Love

1. *Brothers love brothers.*
2. *Brothers listen to brothers.*
3. *Brothers love their teachers.*
4. *Brothers share with other brothers.*
5. *Brothers respect their teachers.*
6. *Brothers respect other brothers.*
7. *Brothers do their work in class before they play.*
8. *Brothers listen to their teachers.*

The "Brother-Law" and "Brother-Love" pledges were something we recited every morning before we got our day started and it resonated well with them. It was the first time that anybody had told them that their friends or classmates were their brothers and that they should treat and love them as such. For the most part, many Black boys are sent to school with the message that if somebody hits you, you hit them back. I am not opposed to self-defense. However, my message to them was that it was normal to have differences, argue or sometimes even fight, but that the person they were arguing and fighting with was their brother and not their enemy. Having them view of each other as their brothers instead of enemies was cultivating *love* between them instead of *hatred*.

When I was their age and as I grew into becoming a teenager, I considered guys I had fights with as my natural born enemies. I would have never considered them as my brothers, because I wasn't taught to consider them as my brothers. I believe if I had been afforded that education of self and kinship, it would have impacted me in a very positive way. I wouldn't have wanted to be violent towards guys who were my brothers and I wouldn't have viewed them as enemies and dealt with them as such. I was committed to educating my students differently than the way I was educated on how to handle conflicts at their age.

I took my class to gym one day and other classes were in there playing as well. It was close to 40 students in the gym with about six teachers. One of the teachers left out of the gym and the rest of us were trying to watch his class as well as our own. I was standing on the side playing with a group of my students and I noticed a student of the teacher who had left, playing by an electric socket. Before I knew it, he had stuck something into the electric socket and was electrocuted! I ran over there and knocked his hand away from the socket before it could kill him. If I had not reached him when I did, his injuries could have been fatal. I didn't think twice about my decision to run over there to save him, even though I was risking my own life. I knew his life was in jeopardy and it was my responsibility as a human being to save him. Sacrifices are necessary for the betterment of our communities. All of the staff in the gym was suspended with pay and the teacher who left the gym was fired.

I used my time on suspension to finish writing my book. While I was writing my book, I decided to record a soundtrack and film a documentary as well. I had no idea how I was going to accomplish it, because I didn't know anybody in either field. What I did know was that I wanted to get it done, by any means necessary. I eventually reached out to a producer and he invited me to his studio inside of a shoeshine parlor. I sat there for about three hours and he was a no show. There were others artists waiting to record with him as well. A woman kept looking at me funny the whole time I was there so, I eventually began a conversation with her. I learned her name was Tab and that she was an R&B singer working on her album with one of the best producers in Detroit. I met with her a few more times over the next couple of weeks and did my best to recruit her to help me record my soundtrack. During one of our meetings I learned that the reason that she was looking at me funny the day I met her was because she thought I was crazy as hell with my hair all over my head. I had long locks, which many people call "dreadlocks". I didn't call my hairstyle dreadlocks because I didn't dread my locks. Locks are more than a hairstyle to me. They are a lifestyle which speaks and reflects our heritage and culture as Afrikan people and our spiritual connection to God.

Tab eventually introduced me to her producer Blak Joe and it didn't take a lot to sell him on my project. Tab and I recruited several different artists such as Joe Black, Anna Doll, Mighty O, Money Wellz, Seven the General, Somebody and others to record songs for the soundtrack and Blak Joe provided us with the production. We recruited many virtually unknown artists who didn't have ego issues and who bought into the concept of the project. They were hungry to display their talents to the world. We recorded some of the best music to come out of Detroit in a long time. I eventually met another brother named Shaka and I recruited him to film and edit my documentary. I achieved both on a zero budget.

I decided to use the soundtrack and documentary to promote my book. I organized two premiers for both projects. I did the first one at Black Star Community Bookstore owned by Malik Yakini, who was also a member of HOPE. Malik took me up under his wing as a long time Detroit activist and became one of my biggest supporters. Malik is one of the most respected community activists in the City of Detroit so; I considered it an honor to be able to learn from him and to have his support. The first premier was standing room only and I did the second one at the famous King Solomon Church located in my neighborhood, Zone 8. This is the church where Malcolm X delivered his famous speech, "Message to the Grassroots" in 1963. With the help of Charles Simmons and his wife Mama Sandra, we were able to pack the church out. Charles Simmons and his wife were Directors of the community based museum, Hush House which is located right around the corner from my mama's house, also in Zone 8. The museum displays actual pictures, books and other artifacts from the Civil Rights and Black Power Movements as well as other aspects of Black history. Each time I go into the Hush House, it is better than the last time I visited and I learn something new.

Charles Simmons is a professor at Eastern Michigan University "EMU" and also teaches at Marygrove College and Wayne County Community College "WCCC". He specializes in journalism at these prestigious colleges. Mama Sandra teaches at Wayne State University "WSU" in the English department. When my book came out, they were the first professors to use it in their respected classes at EMU, WCCC and WSU. They also invited me to speak to the college students during different events they hosted at the Hush House. They adopted me as their son and have supported me unconditionally as a son and as an activist.

During my premier at King Solomon church, we watched the documentary first, which was real and raw and exposed the anger, pain and hurt of Black males surviving in third world neighborhood conditions in Detroit. After watching the documentary, I spoke immediately after it and took questions from the audience. When we

92

were breaking things down, a white guy came up to me and said, "If I had just watched the documentary, I would have thought one way, but after listening to you speak after the documentary, it was compelling and powerful. You should bottle this up and package it everywhere." I appreciated the positive feedback.

At work things were getting crazy because we weren't getting paid on time. We all knew something was up, but we had no idea what it was. It eventually came out that our Director was accused of mismanaging Head Start funds and embezzlement. She was removed from her position while she was being investigated. Things were even more hectic because we knew that many of us would not be returning in the fall.

One morning I got up as usual and went through my normal routine of getting ready for work. When I walked outside, I noticed that my car had been stolen. Even though I was pissed about my car, I was more pissed about possibly missing work. Although I had worked there for over a year and was considered a hard worker, I had never stopped walking on eggshells. In the back of my mind, I could be called into the office at any time and be fired because I was a convicted felon. That was a social nightmare that I lived with at every job I worked. So, instead of missing work, I pulled my bike out of my basement and started pedaling my way to work. I did that every day until I saved up enough money to purchase another car. Many of my co-workers thought I was crazy, because I was riding my bike from the Westside to the Eastside of Detroit without any hesitation. In hindsight, I was crazy! I was crazy enough to do whatever it took to keep my job, because as a convicted felon, jobs don't come easy for us!

Writing my book came easy for me. I started in November of 2006 and was done writing it in April of 2007. My next step was to get it edited, have the book cover designed and raise the money to publish it. Unfortunately, I was running into a lot of different road blocks from family and friends. People couldn't overstand why I wanted to write a

93

book and were discouraging me at every corner I turned, about following my dream. I was surrounded by so much doubt that I even started to doubt myself.

One morning I woke up completely frustrated and decided to cut off my long beautiful locks. Cutting my hair was a *metaphor* for cutting all the fake people out of my life and the new growth would be the new people I would meet that would help me to achieve my goals. At that time in my life, I had to dig deep inside the depths of my soul in order to find the guts to believe in myself and in order to overcome all the doubt that I was surrounded by. That doubt had began to take root inside of me and I knew I had to change that.

What I learned during that process was that others will doubt you, criticize you and even question you as if you don't know what you are doing. The challenge is for you not to doubt yourself, criticize yourself or question yourself as if you shouldn't follow your dreams/goals. Once you start to believe other's doubts of you over your own confidence in yourself, you are doomed and have destroyed the foundation of putting your best foot forward. The challenges we encounter in life offer opportunities for growth, development and motivation to move beyond the negative and focus on the positive. We overcome obstacles by going within ourselves to tap into our strength to go around them, through them, over them or even under them in order to stay the course. It is our undying belief in ourselves, which inspires us to push forward against whatever odds stand in our way. We have to love ourselves enough to never give up on ourselves, no matter how much people doubt us. Self-love is a strong enough force to inspire anyone to achieve their goals and to follow their dreams. As long as we remember that we all are born out of struggle and we embrace our struggles, we can make it do what it do! You hold the key to your own vision, goals and dreams, so don't be afraid to live for them and do what it takes to achieve them.

When I got back to work with my new look, many of my co-workers were coming up to me and speaking, but didn't even know my name. Having locks and my demeanor scared the hell of out of many of them. After cutting my hair, my co-workers felt like I was more approachable, even though I was the same guy, I just had short hair. During this time, Detroit was chosen as the place to host the Head Start National Convention. So, I applied to co-facilitate with Shawn White, who had worked at Wayne County Head Start, but had branched out to do her own thing. As things were looking up for her, she reached back for me to co-facilitate the workshop, because she was one of the few people who recognized my talents and potential early on. The workshop was titled, "Fatherhood the Blueprint". Shawn ended up arriving late because of traffic, but I'm proud to say that I did a pretty good job holding things down until she arrived. It was the first major workshop that I had conducted and we had a packed room in both sessions. I was extremely proud of myself after that and was grateful to Shawn for asking me to co-facilitate the workshop with her.

I decided to release my book on my mama's birthday in 2008. It was my way of showing my appreciation for her numerous sacrifices for me over the years. I was excited about the publication and release of my book, because it ultimately became a team project with my comrads and father. The editing was done by my comrads Shaka and Greer-Bey, the book cover was done by my comrad Kwasi and the Introduction and Epilogue were written by my comrad Shaka and my father Baruti. The book displayed the talents of formerly incarcerated men and those still incarcerated and showcased them as writers, editors and graphic designers. More importantly, these were skills we all taught ourselves, which sent an even more important message. Once I released my book, I had no idea what new challenges I would be confronted with. I went back to every person and organization I had worked with and told them about the release of my book, but I received little support. I then went to all the bookstores in Detroit and asked them about carrying my book on their shelves, but they all gave me the run around except Source Books, Hood Books and Black Star Community Bookstore. Despite those bookstores and folks giving me the cold shoulder, I kept pushing forward. I had tunnel vision and was determined to succeed. I was committed and armed with a refuse to lose mindset so, I was able to I

95

rely on my prison experience to get through that difficult time. I recognized that if I could make it through that hellhole, I could make it through anything!

One day while I was at work, I was sent to fill in at another site for a staff member that had left work early for being sick. I arrived right after nap time. When I got there, one of my co-workers asked me if I minded if she brought one of her male students to my class who was being real disruptive. I said I wouldn't mind. He was in the corner playing with another student and he asked me if he could call me dad. I was like sure. It was my first time ever meeting this little boy. When his mother came to pick him up, I explained to her what had happened. That incident confirmed in my mind, the desperate need for strong male role models in our community then and now.

At work I would learn that my fear of not returning in the fall was warranted. I was initially shell shocked, because I didn't know what I was going to do next. I was used to receiving a paycheck every two weeks and my livelihood depended upon that paycheck. Luckily, I would realize that being laid off was the best thing that could have happened to me. Out of an unexpected negative came a real positive. Overnight I went from working for someone to working for myself. It afforded me an opportunity to reinvent myself and *re-imagine* what work meant to me as a human being, while at the same time keeping my commitment to being a *change agent* for my community. Up to that point I had never thought about being an entrepreneur and had never taken a business class in my life. In prison I had *studied* world politics, world religion and world history, but nothing related to business. Out of *necessity,* I transformed myself into a businessman, author and speaker. I named my company Urban Guerilla Entertainment, because the term "Urban Guerrilla" symbolized what I embodied as a man who had a souljah mentality engaging in a war for my livelihood, through serving my community in order to make it better. I was on a mission despite the many odds that stood in my way. Once I realized my greatest asset was my experience, I dissected it as a student and emerged with a PhD in the survival of urban amerikkka. I was able to articulate my experiences passionately and with the best of them. I had 1000 books that needed to be sold and I felt very strongly that my story was a story that amerikkka needed to hear and read. It was an epic journey of hope, triumph, redemption and transformation between a father and a son in prison and it told one of the most dynamic, honest, compelling and thought-provoking stories of the 21st century. So, I went about the business of selling my books and working for myself.

One morning I was driving in my car listening to 107.5 FM in Detroit and radio personality John Mason "Mason" announced that he and his team would be at the famous Motown Museum every Saturday celebrating the glory days of Motown. Since Motown was located in my neighborhood Zone 8, I decided to go one Saturday and give Mason a copy of my book. When I got there it was pretty packed so, I waited patiently in line during the break to introduce myself to him. I told him I was from the neighborhood and co-founded the gang Zone 8, which ultimately led to my imprisonment for a crime I did not commit. I also told him that I had met my father for the first time while in prison. After listening to me, he responded by saying he would love to have me on his show for an interview next week. Meeting Mason went better than expected. I never anticipated that he was going to invite me on his show right on the spot. I was just hoping that he would take my book, read it and then be inspired to interview me. I was totally caught off guard, but was super excited about the opportunity that was presented before me. He told me to come down to the station the following Tuesday at 8:30AM so, I was there at 8:00AM. Since I have been home, I have always made it my business to arrive to any meeting or job interview at least 30 minutes ahead of time. This has earned me a lot of respect from the people I've had meetings with and from those who have chosen to hire me.

Mason asked me before we went on the air if there was anything specific that I wanted to talk about. I replied no and that my life was an open book so, I was open to talking about anything. When we went on the air, I just opened up and bared my soul to his listeners. I shared my story of redemption and transformation through meeting my father in prison and spoke completely from my heart. I blew Mason and his listeners away with my honest and heartfelt responses to his questions. He had booked me for his 15 minutes of fame segment, but the interview went on for 25 minutes. After the interview Mason gave me his personal cell phone number, the direct line to the radio station and conveyed to me that anytime I was doing anything, to call him and he would bring me on the air to promote it. Since that day I have been a guest on his show over 50 times and he never charged me a dime! While I was on the air, I gave my number out so that people who wanted to contact me could buy my book. By the time I reached my car, I had over 20 voicemail messages from people who had heard me on the radio. Once I got in my car, I continued to receive more phone calls from people expressing how proud they were of me. I was so overwhelmed with all the phone calls that I had to pull over to take it all in. Never in my lifetime had I had so many people tell me how proud they were of me. I just pulled over and started crying, because I was moved by the phone calls from all the people who had been moved by hearing my story.

Mason responded to his listeners by saying, "This man is the example and reason why you should never throw anybody away. God has blown his power into him so he can touch others." He went on to say, "I have listened to scholars that till this day still have not explained or broken down the issues and offered solutions as Yusef did in 25 minutes. This man is giving solutions to problems that no one else seems to be able to put into words. This man teaches our babies, from prison to the classrooms! What an incredible story and man!"

Mason became one of my biggest supporters and never denied me an opportunity to go on his show and promote a community event I had organized or was speaking at. He gave me the break I needed, by exposing me to *thousands of listeners* not only here in Detroit, but statewide and across the nation. I became a household name after being on his show and sold hundreds of books to listeners that heard me on his program. Mason is a different type of radio personality, because he still has his fingers on the pulse of the people. I consider him a radio activist which is a dying breed amongst Black radio hosts. To make it more blunt, I met another famous Detroit radio host and I gave them one of my books at a community event. One day I was out at a store shopping and ran into one of my former head start parents. She congratulated me on my book and I immediately asked her how she got a copy. She responded by saying that her sister was interning for a radio personality and that the radio personality had her throw it out. However, instead of her sister throwing it away, she decided to keep it. As the old saying goes "one man's trash is another man's treasure".

Mason hosted the "Mason in the Morning Show" on WJLB 97.9 FM in Detroit for 18 years. He eventually moved on to host another radio show on 102.7 FM Kiss-FM/WDMK. He then left there and reemerged as the independent owner of his own morning show called "Mason Radio, Inc." Mason was the only morning show personality in a major market to *own* his *own show* and his show was syndicated. In October of 2011, Mason's radio program abruptly came to an end when Radio One assumed operating responsibility of WGPR 107.5FM. The new owners decided to cancel his show. Losing Mason's voice over the radio airwaves is a tragedy in Detroit, because what Black radio has become is a larger tragedy across this country. Mason was one of the last radio personalities that hadn't sold out the people by feeding them garbage. He used his radio program to empower and educate his listeners with the music he played and the many interviews he conducted. I will forever be grateful to John Mason for being the first person to allow my voice and story to be heard on a major radio station. Thank you and I love you brother!

After being on Mason's show, I got a phone call from a brother named Leon Jones. He was the lead singer of a gospel group called Resurrection. He had also been to prison, but had been home for over 20 years and was actively involved in making a difference in Detroit. He reached out to me to be on a community panel about changing the culture of violence in our youth. My participation was well received by the audience and he thanked me for my contribution. He also informed me that he would be calling me in the future to continue to work with him on other community events.

As the summer of 2008 was progressing, I decided to organize another school supply give away in my neighborhood Zone 8. I reconnected with the organizations I had previously worked with, such as Wayne Metro Head Start and HOPE and they supported my efforts. I also came out of my own pocket. We organized the event within three weeks and gave away brand new clothes and school supplies to the neighborhood youth. The event was called, "State of Emergency of the Urban Youth". I did the event at my mama's house, which allowed me to eliminate an overhead and to impact my neighborhood, which was dear to my heart. Even though the event was successful in meeting a need in our community, I knew there was a lot more work that needed to be done. People in neighborhoods like Zone 8 in Detroit were given up on and left for dead a long time ago. They began to give up on themselves and to roam their neighborhoods like zombies. They began to adopt a non-caring attitude which was reflected in their behavior towards each other and even towards themselves through violent tendencies. This non-caring attitude is rooted in their being *betrayed* and *sold out* continuously after investing their hope, faith and trust into fake ass politicians, pastors, business folks and community leaders who take their hope, faith and trust and exploit it for their own personal gain. This has helped to shape the hopelessness and helplessness that some people are buried alive in today.

Over 150 people came out to the event, but I was determined to make it even bigger and better the following year. I learned my activism and organizing skills from my mother. Being an activist is at the heart of being a parent, by advocating on behalf of your children every day of your lives until they know how to advocate on behalf of themselves and even after. Not only did my mother advocate for her children, but she advocated for others by opening her doors to feed those who were hungry and providing a bed for those who were homeless. My mama gave me the reference to be the activist I am today.

I never realized that writing my book would provide me with a platform to stand on, by making my voice and my message that much stronger. It made it so that people would have to take notice of me. I just needed to learn how to make it work for me. I had nobody walking me through the early part of the process so; I was forced to figure it out on my own. Those people that did notice me often viewed me as a threat and treated me like I was a *social cancer*. When I emerged as a speaker, many people and organizations wouldn't book me for speaking engagements so, I did the next best thing and started organizing my own community events. My events would focus on numerous urban issues and I would book myself as the keynote speaker. After one of my events, a "Peace and Justice Summit," a white guy came up to me and said he was impressed after hearing me speak so, he wanted to help me. He invited me out to dinner to meet other local Black activists who were doing work in the community. After he introduced me at dinner, two Black women at the table started drilling me and asking me how they were supposed to know that I had actually changed. I responded as passionately as I possibly could and with just as much conviction by saying, "by the fact that I am not outside waiting to rob one of you muthafuckers!" That was the end of that conversation and we proceeded to eat our dinner.

More frequently, people were starting to invite me to be involved with different panels, events and meetings, but when I would get there they wanted me to be a *fly* on the wall. However, once I opened up my mouth, I became an *elephant* in the room. My book was picking up momentum and I was organizing and speaking all across the City. I slowly but surely, began to grow into a force to be reckoned with in the City of Detroit, because of my book, speaking and community organizing and activism. Some people may not have liked what I said, but they damn sure had to respect me, because I was working my ass off and had earned the respect and admiration of the people. The same thing could be said about my book. Some people may not have agreed with what I wrote, but they respected the honest way in which I conveyed my thoughts on paper. Having the support of the people allowed me to navigate through the *old guard* which was attempting to box me out or make me into a *foot soldier* for one of them. Instead of being *co-opted*, I remained one of the few *independent voices* in the City of Detroit and spoke for the true interest of the people. I still remain that way even to this day! This *old guard* is in the fucking way, suffocating the people with old ideas and outdated leadership! This is not only a local problem, but a national problem! We desperately need new, young and vibrant leadership to be ushered in, who are rooted in knowing the past, are prepared to organize the people through proactive programs and are willing to seize victory in the future.

As promised, I received a phone call from Leon Jones. He asked me to meet him at Fellowship Chapel Church so that we could appear on Rev. Wendell Anthony's local weekly TV show "To the Point". It would be my first time meeting Rev. Anthony who was also the President of the NAACP's Detroit Chapter. He was so impressed after hearing my story that he bought a book from me. A few weeks later I received a phone call from Teferi Brent a long time Detroit activist, who was also member of Fellowship Chapel Church and he mentioned to me that Rev. Anthony had given a sermon during church service about my story. I was speechless.

I would eventually join Fellowship Chapel Church, because I respected the things that they were doing in the community through the work led by Teferi Brent, Derek Blackmon, Joe Baker (RIP) and others. I was the featured speaker for their annual Men's Week program in front of about 100 church members and community people, and was well received by the audience. To my surprise, the next day at church I was awarded with the "Rev. Wendell Anthony Social Activist Award of 2008". At the time, I would only be the second person to receive that award and it would be my first community award. After paying my dues, I had blossomed into a solid community activist and organizer, who was well respected locally and nationally.

You may find a person who speaks more eloquently and dresses more professionally than I do, but you'd be hard pressed to find a person with a more genuine heart, who represents the realness of hope, redemption and transformation and who works as hard as I do on behalf of the people. My presentation is a bit more polished these days, but I am still the raw and real person that I was years ago.

Me & DeAngelo when I first came home from prison.

When I was sent back to prison...I was mad as hell!!!

MICHIGAN
DEPARTMENT OF
CORRECTIONS
JAN 26 2001
223605
PRISONER

RUFFIN, JOSEPH

Me & DeAngelo visiting my dad for the first time.

Me & my dad visiting.

Me & Kobie.

Me & my family.

Me graduating from college.

Me when I was working at Highland Park Head Start.

Me when I was working at Southeast Head Start with all male students.

106

Me with General Baker

Me with Marian Kramer & Chrystal who I taught in Head Start.

The first community event I helped organized called "Young Brothas & Sistas on a Move in 2003 in Z8ne. At the bottom, me recognizing Mother Feebie for her community work & me giving away free school clothes to a youth from the neighborhood.

Cicero Love, Fred Hampton Jr. & myself in D.C. at the 10 yr anniversary of the Million Man March.

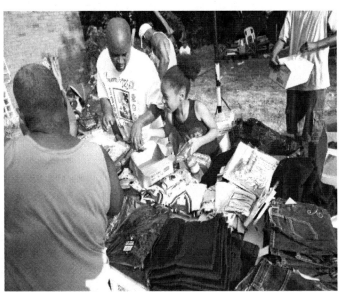

1st year of the annual back to school supply in Z8ne

2nd year of the annual back to school supply in Z8ne.

Me & Kwasi at the 3rd year of the annual school supply in Z8ne.

We had over 300 people come & support. It was a great day in Z8ne/Detroit.

4th year of the school supply giveaway. In 4 yrs we have given away over 1,000 backpacks filled with school supplies. Our sponsors has been HOPE, City Councilman Ken Cockrel Jr., CVS, A&H Contractors, Bank of America, Urban Network & Urban Guerrilla Ent.

9 Years In — 9 Years Out

Chapter 9

I continued my ground level activism efforts by addressing the many social ills that were plaguing Detroit neighborhoods. During my efforts, I united with a person that I admired and respected named Allen Martin. He was a long time Detroit activist, who had appeared on numerous local and national radio and television programs including "Dateline", "20/20" and the "Tom Joyner Morning Show" for his efforts to curb youth violence. He was the founder of the organization "Take Back Our City (TBOC)" which worked exclusively with gangs in efforts to reduce violence and homicides. Allen's views and my views complimented each other very well and I was excited about the opportunity to learn from a veteran activist. He admired and respected me too and never hesitated to indicate how much I reminded him of one of his late mentees. The passion, energy and conviction that I embodied drew him back into doing what he loved, which was working on the ground level. I considered that a huge compliment and it further solidified the fact that I was doing the right thing with my life.

Unfortunately, it had become quite obvious that shit was going to get worse before it got better in Detroit. So, Allen and I decided to go downtown to speak with City Councilwoman JoAnn Watson. We expressed to her that if we didn't take immediate action; bodies were going to start piling up in the streets of Detroit at a rapid rate. After listening to us intensely, Councilwoman Watson agreed to join our efforts and we formed the "Peace & Justice Task Force". In October of 2008, we presented the task force before the Detroit City Council to be voted on as a resolution. It passed without a problem, but the real challenge came when we needed to secure funding and support for the work that needed to be done in order to decrease youth violence in Detroit. Sadly, although the "Peace & Justice Task Force" represented great promise, it never came into fruition, because money was never made available to support it.

When the Kwame Kilpatrick *scandal* made national news, Detroit became the laughing stock of the nation. The *scandal* buried Detroiters in *shame* and *embarrassment* and divided the city. Folks were

112

either pro-Kwame or anti-Kwame. There seemed to be no middle ground. In my estimate, Kwame was a politician so, he behaved like one. The only difference was that he was Black so the *mass media* treated his poor decision making and arrogance different than they treated the white politicians who mastered the political corruption he got caught up in. Long before Kwame was elected as Mayor of Detroit, there was political corruption and politicians cheating on their wives. However, none of them had ever been attacked by the *mass media* like he was. It became obvious that his attacks were *rooted* in institutional racism and open racism, but make no mistake about it, *my aim is not to defend* Kwame or to *make excuses for his behavior*. I am just putting things into perspective. There have been white politicians across this country that have done a lot worse things than Kwame, because keep in mind that he has not been convicted of anything criminal to date. In 2005, "Time Magazine" proclaimed to the world that he was the worst Mayor in any big city and this was three years before his scandal became public knowledge. They never deemed Bill Clinton the worst President for having a staff member perform oral sex on him in the white house or any other white politician who has stolen money, lied and cheated the people they were elected to serve.

The issue I have with Kwame is that he was supposed to *represent* the best of us and he jacked that off. He *abused* our trust, *exploited* our faith and made us all look *stupid* for supporting him. More importantly, he took the aspirations, dreams and hopes of thousands of Black boys in the City of Detroit and *flushed* them down the toilet by destroying his career with arrogance, stupidity and poor decision making. His actions set Black men in the City of Detroit back decades. Through all of this, I can say that a very important lesson has been learned. A great deal of responsibility comes with talent, potential, charisma, good looks and knowledge. So, when you have those things, people will depend on you and look up to you. *I will forever cherish that lesson.*

Also in the wake of the Kilpatrick scandal was the Detroit Public School (DPS) *debacle*. Michigan Governor, Jennifer Granholm brought in Emergency Financial Manager, Robert Bobb to oversee DPS. He launched a full blown assault, closing dozens of schools and laying off dozens of teachers and other DPS staff members, adding further chaos to a school system already in shambles. The Kwame scandal had us bathing in shame and the Bobb madness had us running around like chickens with our heads cut off. Yes, DPS was a fucked up shit-uation long before Bobb arrived, but by the time he left, the shit-uation was even worse. One of the greatest mistakes Bobb made was to merge rival schools. He either didn't take into account the history of the school rivalries or he just didn't care. Either way, his actions were negligent and irresponsible. Only a *madman* would merge schools notorious for being violent towards one another. Rival gang members were placed under the same roof and expected to learn without incident, *Yeah right*! He was not only doing this to high school students, but he was also forcing elementary and middle school students to attend schools outside of their neighborhoods. His method of "dealing with" the DPS system, created a hectic shit-uation for Detroit households on every level.

Henry Ford High School located on the Westside of Detroit, was merged with its well known rival, Redford High School. It was no secret to DPS or the Detroit Police Department (DPD) that these two schools were enemies. Redford High School was formerly housed directly across the street from what used to be known as the Eighth Police Precinct so nothing that occurred at Redford High School was much of a secret from DPD. Shortly after the merger of the two schools, there was a shooting outside of Henry Ford High School and when the smoke cleared, a student had been murdered. Predictably, everybody was in an up roar about it even though the writing had always been on the wall. For whatever reason, nobody paid attention to the time bomb waiting to happen between Henry Ford and Redford High Schools. This incident inspired Allen Martin and I to petition the City Council to support our plan of action for dealing with youth violence. Not only had over 50 DPS schools been closed, but numerous recreation centers had been closed as well, creating a chaotic shit-uation on the streets of Detroit. Closing these institutions was easy for decision makers, because they didn't live in the neighborhoods that would be negatively impacted by their choices, nor did their children attend those schools or recreation centers. There was no danger to their families.

Crime and violence in urban cities across amerikkka, especially Detroit, has become *recreational* for urban youth. Many of them find fun in robbing, gang banging, slanging and murdering because that *death-style* has captured their imagination as a way of life. Unfortunately, political and religious leadership over cities like Detroit put the nail in the coffin when they cut off alternative options, such as recreation

114

centers. This leaves the youth with one alternative, which is the streets and once the streets get a hold of their young impressionable minds, they become subjected to those who only value *MONEY, MACK* and *MURDER*!

During this period, Mason was broadcasting live once a week at the Motown Casino. I went there to promote an event I was doing and met former Deputy Mayor, Freeman Hendrix. He worked directly under former Mayor, Dennis Archer and had run against Kwame during his second term, but came up short in the 12th round. Hendrix decided to throw his name back into the hat after the scandal so, we talked about his candidacy. He indicated to me that he had an issue with the fact that former prisoners did not have equal rights. Of course, this held my attention so, I listened to him intently. When he was done talking, he invited me to speak at a Youth Summit that was going to be held at Northwestern High School to address youth violence. I was excited about the opportunity to speak at Northwestern, because it was located in Zone 8 and many of the youth there were claiming Zone 8. He also gave me a lot to think about with regard to supporting him in the Mayoral race against Dave Bing, Warren Evans and Ken Cockrel Jr.

Even though I had never met any of the candidates, the only two I was considering supporting was him or Ken Cockrel Jr. and I was most skeptical about supporting Hendrix. When he was Deputy Mayor, he called the police and had a grandmother forcefully removed from a school board meeting so, this did not sit well with me. However, after talking with different people, I became convinced that he was a changed man. More importantly, he convinced me that he was serious about and would make it a priority to address the many discriminatory issues that men and women who returned home from prison faced. Also, my decision to work with Freeman Hendrix reflected my attitude that I was willing to work with anybody in order to improve Detroit.

Unfortunately, just minutes before the Youth Summit was to begin at Northwestern High School, it was cancelled. Many of the participants including, but not limited to, local rappers, gang squad police, Freeman Hendrix, radio personality Reggie Reg Davis and Mouchettee Muhammad, circled up in the back of the school trying to figure out why it had been cancelled. When I approached the group, Freeman Hendrix introduced me as a co-founding member of the gang

Zone 8 and advised them that he had invited me. Some of the people there had already heard of me. Once the group began to disperse, Reggie Reggie and I began to talk. I explained my story to him and he bought a book from me. Shortly after that day, I received a phone call from Reggie Reg about appearing on his weekly radio show on 102.7 FM. He was blown away by the transformation I had made in my life by graduating from college and becoming an activist after having served prison time. He was also intrigued by the fact that I had met my father in prison and that he was the cause for my redemption. I was invited to be a guest on his show numerous times after that.

I would learn from Reggie Reg that the Youth Summit had been rescheduled for Henry Ford High School where the young man had recently been murdered. Although it was obvious that moving the Youth Summit from Northwestern to Henry Ford was a purely political decision, I decided to attend after an invitation from Reggie Reg and much deliberation. Deciding to move past the politics and attend the summit was one of the best decisions I had made to date. When I got there, the atmosphere was intense between the parents from that neighborhood and the politicians. The parents were pissed and didn't appreciate being force fed bullshit by politicians. I was sitting up front and was ready to leave until this tall dark skinned man began to talk. What he was saying resonated with me, because he wasn't pulling any punches about the *state of violence* in the City of Detroit. Plus, I recognized him from somewhere, but could not remember where. When he walked past me after he was finished speaking, it hit me like a ton of bricks and I recalled where I knew him from. I had seen him in the episode of *American Gangster* where they highlighted the drug family the "Chamber Brothers". I was all in watching it after I learned that the hit movie *New Jack City* had been based upon one of the Chamber Brothers' drug spots on Detroit's Eastside and that he had been a consultant for the movie. His breakdown of urban violence and urban cities captivated me. When he described urban cities as third world cities, it stuck with me immediately and I never forgot it. So, when he walked by me, I got up and followed him out into the hallway. He was standing up against the wall by himself and I had no idea that he wasn't feeling well. I walked up to him and introduced myself and he responded by telling me that his name was Carl S. Taylor. I knew I only had a few minutes of his time so, I quickly conveyed to him who I was and gave

116

him one of my books. He accepted my book, but gave me a look that said, "Who is this guy?"

At that time, it still had not registered with me that Carl was a heavy weight, not only nationally, but internationally for researching and dealing with youth violence. He was also a Professor of Sociology at Michigan State University. A few days went by and I received an email from Carl that said, "I finished it, wow, it is so strong, real, great work, full of truth, it should be a book in every juvenile center. Let me help you get this more attention. I will return on Wednesday, call my office around three thirty." When Wednesday came, I called him and we talked like we had known each other all of our lives. He was real and very down to earth, but brutally honest. He said, "I wasn't feeling well and I was thinking, who the hell is this young guy walking up to me? Then you gave me a book and I get books all the time, but when I read it, it moved me." From that conversation, Carl became a father figure, big brother, friend and mentor in my life. One day he drove to Detroit from Lansing and invited me to lunch with him and his brother Al, who also embraced me as a little brother. Over lunch he conveyed to me, "negro I support you because you are on the streets making it happen and just know I will always keep it real with you and I expect the same thing from you. We are not going to agree every time, but as long as we understand that, we will be fine. Hands down you are one of the hardest working men in Detroit making something out of nothing and I respect that!"

Meeting Carl was another breakthrough for me, because he was a man that was world renowned, but never forgot his roots as a native Detroiter. He was reaching back to teach me what he had learned from his own journey in amerikkka as a Black man and I knew it was no easy task. I recognized that he couldn't possibly assist every person that approaches him so, I was grateful that I had impacted him in a way that inspired him to want to make a positive contribution to my life.

Carl S. Taylor, PhD is a professor in the Department of Sociology, Senior Fellow in University Outreach and Engagement and MSU Extension Specialist at Michigan State University. He has extensive experience in field research aimed at the reduction of violence involving amerikkkan youth. He has taught in the school of Criminal Justice at Michigan State University and at Grand Valley State University. He has directed the Department of Criminal Justice and

117

Public Safety at Jackson Community College, served as a clinical professor to the Grand Valley State University Criminal Justice and Police Academy and as an Associate of the National Community Policing Center. He has also worked with communities, foundations and government agencies to contribute to the understanding of gangs, youth culture and violence. Having conducted research projects in Detroit over the last two decades, he has a strong overstanding of the problems facing many neighborhoods in urban amerikkka. Two projects involving urban gangs have resulted in books summarizing the up close and personal impact of violence on communities: *Dangerous Society* and *Girls, Gangs, Women, and Drugs*, both published by Michigan State University Press. *Jugendkulturen und Gangs (Youth Culture and Gangs)*, published in Germany, extends his study internationally.

As 2008 was coming to an end, I wanted to bring in the New Year with a bang by introducing the second edition of my new book. I decided to ask Carl to write a new Foreword for my book and he responded by saying that it would be an honor to write it. Carl's endorsement of my book with the new Foreword was powerful and it meant a lot to me. When I decided to write it, I never thought about going to a publishing company to have them publish it. I strongly felt in the beginning that it was my duty to give birth to my project and I was proud to watch it grow. Also, I believed that it didn't make sense to ask someone to invest in me when I hadn't shown them that I had invested in myself. Even though I lived my story, I felt in my heart that it was my responsibility to bring my story to the world. So, when I would find myself at the table with different folks, I wasn't asking them to help me get my book published, because I did that and they respected me for it. They were also more willing to help me, because they saw a man that was on a mission, by any means necessary.

During this time, Reggie Reg had recruited me to be a part of the organization "Cease Fire", which he had founded with Mouchettee Muhammad of the Nation of Islam here in Detroit. It was founded in order to address the youth violence in DPS, because he was inspired to do something after the death of his young brother years earlier. We toured over 50 different DPS schools and I spoke and shared my story with the youth. I would generally get at least 10 youth asking for books after I spoke and I would always accommodate them. Afterwards, many of the youth would call and tell me how reading my book had changed

118

their life. Or, if I ran into one of them, they would express how much they loved reading my book and how it had challenged them to change their life. Many adults, teachers and school administrators believe students don't voluntarily read, but what they fail to overstand is that the youth will read what's relevant to them. They want to read something that they can relate to and that is what my book provides. When I speak to youth, I tell them that I see who I used to be, but through me, they can see who they could be, minus my many mistakes. I let them know that God has granted me a second chance to help them realize their first chance.

Soon after, I ran into Madeline Hardgest, a woman I had previously worked with at another program. I hadn't seen her in a few years so; she invited me over to her office located on the corner of Woodward and West Grand Blvd to catch up. When I arrived, I brought her up to speed regarding my life and gave her a copy of my book. She then invited me to a graduation celebration for a class of men who had been through prison job training that she oversaw, scheduled for later that day. By the time I got there, I had forgotten which floor the event was on. I took the elevator up to the wrong floor and an older man in a suit got on with me. We got off on the same floor to attend the event, but we had about 20 minutes left before it started so, we talked a bit. He asked me what I did for a living and I told him about the work I had been doing in the community since my release from prison and that I was an author. He was fascinated by my story, but was even more thrilled by what I had been able to accomplish against incredible odds and with little help from any prison re-entry programs. He walked me over to the corner and drilled me with question after question and I answered them openly and honestly. The more questions I answered, the more he was impressed with me. He bought my book and then asked if I would mind being put onto the program and speaking to the audience. I told him that it would be an honor. I had no idea that he was a part owner of the Lake Shore Engineering Building that we were standing in, which was a multi-million dollar company. He was completely behind the program of giving men and women returning home from prison a realistic chance at making a successful transition back into society. I soon learned that his name was Tom Hardiman and that he had grown up on the Northern side of Detroit in a small community that stood between the Westside and the Eastside. By the age of 21, he and his high school sweetheart had three boys and were married and he was taking care of his family on a firefighter's salary. After being laid off, he enrolled into Wayne State University to pursue a Bachelors of Science Degree in Business Administration, which took him 12 years to earn. While attending Wayne State University, he met his future business partner Avinash Rachmale and they would form a dynamic duo that would take Detroit and the world by storm.

With the goal to create a company for his sons and to generate jobs for Detroiters, Tom purchased A & H Contractors Inc. in 2003. He serves as the President of A & H, a full service construction firm serving both the public and private sector. His three sons Tom Jr. (TJ), Dorian and Johnny were all around my age and were very down to earth. They treated me as a brother and welcomed me as did Maryland and Latonya Hardiman, as a new member of the A& H Contractors team and they all respected my hard work and determination.

Mr. Hardiman ultimately hired me at Lakeshore Economic Coalition to work with Madeline as a Youth Specialist and Consultant for those who had been to prison. He had a passion for giving back to Detroit in a meaningful way, because like many of us, he had friends who had either died or gone to prison. He always conveyed to an audience that the only thing that made him special was the fact that his parents' unconditional love shielded him from the *social madness* that his friends had fallen prey to. I was instructed by him to develop a youth program so, I had the program written and ready to go within a matter of days. I developed a 10 week youth program entitled "Real Boys, Real Talk and Real Girls, Real Talk". The outline of the program went as follows:

REAL BOYS, REAL TALK & REAL GIRLS, REAL TALK

The Program: Real Boys Real Talk & Real Girls Real Talk is designed to engage youth ages 12 – 17 in a healthy dialogue. The objective is to challenge them through dialogue to examine social, sexual, cultural, educational, economical and political influences on Black youth in urban environments. Through a series of dialogues, the youth will be challenged to examine their thought processes, living conditions and cultural norms that influence their lifestyle. This will be a non-judgmental dialogue and will focus on allowing youth to explore their sub-conscious and conscious thinking. The program is designed to be a free space for youth to evaluate their choices and explore healthy lifestyle alternatives that will allow them to maximize their full potential while developing from boys and girls to ultimately men and women. This program is geared towards being a support system for teens to develop the framework for success.

Week 1) Opening Session/ Mentorship
- *Ice Breaker: Penny for thoughts*
- *Establishing ground rules*
- *Goal: To build a healthy understanding what a mentor is.*
- *Objective: To examine people you may view as a mentor or to find you a mentor.*

Week 2) Hip Hop
- *Goal: To understand the impact and influence that Hip-Hop has on the youth.*
- *Objective: To examine the historical evolution of Hip-Hop and how it can be transformed into a positive force for resurrecting dignity in today's youth.*

Week 3) Educational Goal
- *Goal: To establish a foundation for what our youth expect out of school.*
- *Objective: To have a clear understanding of the importance of not only having a High School education but a College education or a Trade/Skill. Define the manner in which you are going to accomplish this.*

Week 4) Family
- *Goal: To understand your relationship to your family, and your family's relationship to you.*
- *Objective: To examine your relationship between you and your family and what impact and influences it has on you.*

Week 5) Self & Community

121

- *Goal: To understand the concrete relationship between the individual and his or her community.*
- *Objective: What are the standards for yourself and your community; in relation to you both helping each other reach full potential.*

Week 6) Male & Female Relationships
- *Goal: To understand the proper way to engage a male or a female either as a friend or someone you are involved with.*
- *Objective: To examine what attracts a male to a female, and female to a male.*

Week 7) Thugs, Gangstas & Hoe's
- *To question why so many Black youth take pride in such negative terms?*
- *To examine the social and psychological behavior patterns for taking pride in such negative terms.*

Week 8) Finances
- *Goal: To understand the proper way of making legit money vs. making illegal money.*
- *Objective: To establish a foundation of how to save money, create a business plan and aspire to be your own boss.*

Week 9) Prisons & more prisons
- *Goal: To understand the impact of criminal behavior of young Black males and Black females.*
- *Objective: To examine why there are so many Black males & Black females in prison rather than in college.*

Week 10) Black Leaders & Black Leadership
- *Goal: To question what a leader is and what is leadership?*
- *Objective: To examine positive/negative Black leaders and Black leadership from the past to the present and their impact on the Black youth.*

122

Tom Hardiman approved the youth program so; the next challenge was to get the youth to participate. I called Mason and asked him if I could announce the program on his radio show and he agreed. I announced the youth program on the radio and by the end of the day, I had 20 students. We were able to attract youth from all over Detroit and Metro-Detroit and the program was a huge success. When the 10 weeks were over, I organized a graduation ceremony and asked Carl to be the keynote speaker. I knew it was a very important day for the graduating students so; I busted my ass to ensure that the room would be packed with people from the community. We had over 200 people come out and support them and my mama catered the event. All of the students had a blast at the graduation and were grateful for the program. More importantly, they were very appreciative of Mr. Hardiman's willingness to invest his time, commitment and money in them.

Things were definitely starting to progress for me as an author, speaker, community organizer and activist. Ron Scott, a former member of the Black Panther Party's Detroit Chapter and a founding member of the Detroit Coalition Against Police Brutality asked me to speak at the community event for slain a youth, Robert Mitchell who had been tasered to death by Warren police. Ron is one of the few veteran activists who have been able to grow with the times as an activist and I was honored to have him as a father figure and mentor in my life. At the event, I would meet Richard Feldman, a long time activist in his own right who invited me to attend a Detroit City of Hope meeting at the Boggs Center. Richard took me up under his wing as well and has supported me unconditionally. After the meeting, Richard suggested that I leave my book for Grace Lee Boggs to read. She read it and invited me over for a meeting with her. It would be my first time meeting her in person, though I had read her autobiography, "Living for Change."

Meeting Grace was a very humbling experience for me. It seemed surreal to be sitting in the living room speaking with a woman that had been a national and international activist for over 50 years. She had worked alongside national and international activists such as her husband James Boggs, C.L.R. James, Albert B. Cleage, Jr., Malcolm X, Richard and Milton Henry, Max Stanford and many others. James Boggs' resume was just as impressive as his wife's and he was most notable for his classic book, written in 1963, *The American Revolution: Pages from a Negro Worker's Notebook*. In later years, he would play an

123

influential role in the Black Power Movement, not only in Detroit, but across the nation and internationally. Albert B. Cleage, Jr., in the 1960s founded the Black church the "Shrine of the Black Madonna" which is a couple of blocks from where I grew up on Linwood. His church was at the forefront of providing leadership to the citizens of Detroit. The Henry brothers had helped co-found the Republic of New Afrika and was actively at the forefront of the leadership in Detroit as well as across the nation for Black people. All them had come together to organize the "Grassroots Leadership Conference" in 1963, where they brought Malcolm X to speak and where he delivered his famous speech, "Message to the Grassroots." Many of these Detroit activists had worked together in bringing Dr. Martin Luther King to Detroit in 1963 as well to participate in a march down Woodward Ave, where he delivered his famous "I Have a Dream" speech in Detroit before he delivered it in Washington, D.C. Max Stanford had been a high ranking member of the Black organization, the "Revolutionary Action Movement (RAM)" and I had the great honor of meeting him last year when he came to Detroit to sit with Grace.

When I met Grace she was 93 years old. It seems like with each new person that she meets, extra days, months and years are added onto her life. She is mentally sharp with a vision of challenging people to re-spirit, transform and re-imagine themselves as new human beings while building a new world and she still has the fire and passion at 96, of a community activist. Grace became one of my biggest supporters and wrote the first review of my book:

LIVING FOR CHANGE REVIEW (July 12th, 2009)
From Thug 2 Father & Freedom Fighter
By Grace Lee Boggs

If your summer reading includes only one book, I recommend Yusef Shakur's The Window 2 My Soul: My Transformation from a Zone 8 Thug to a Father and a Freedom Fighter. As I talked with Yusef Shakur, I thought of the huge changes that have taken place in the Black community since Richard Wright's Native Son (1940), Ralph Ellison's Invisible Man (1952) and Claude Brown's Manchild in the Promised Land (1965). In the mid-20th century these books alerted Americans to the rage against racism that was smoldering in Black ghettos and, as

124

Black youth were being made expendable by Hi-Tech, had begun to explode in the urban rebellions of the 1960s.

Window 2 My Soul is the 21st century story of a new generation of "Outsiders," born since the 60s. This street force, Jimmy Boggs wrote, "compels every member of the Black community, on pain of extinction, to face up to the failure of all institutions in modern America: the economic system, the schools, the welfare system, the hospitals, the police, the political system, i.e. the entire American way of life and to develop a perspective for the total revolutionizing of America."

Window 2 My Soul is not "literature" like Native Son and Invisible Man. Yusef Shakur has coined new words like "shit-uation" and "overstand" to open our eyes to the world of single mothers and absent fathers into which he was born. His mother was 15. He was named Joseph Lee Ruffin after his mother's father. His own father, Richard Lee Carter, 17, had left for the Navy. To provide food, clothing and shelter for him and his sister (by another man), JoJo's mother sold her body to men who used her as a punching bag. She became an alcoholic but never stopped caring for him. Growing up on the mean streets of Detroit where factory jobs had disappeared and crack was king; JoJo's education came from the thugs and predators in Zone 8 (Detroit 48208). So it was natural for him to believe that preying on one another and meeting violence with violence was the way to survive. He was only able to "rebuild himself from the inside out" (p.82) after he was incarcerated (for a crime he did not but could have committed) and was schooled in prison by his father, who had been incarcerated when JoJo was 10 and had overcome self-hate by becoming a Muslim.

Window 2 my Soul is the story of an "Outsider" rebuilding, redefining, re-spiriting himself. It may not be read as widely as Native Son, Invisible Man and Manchild. But I recommend it to anyone seeking to "overstand" our "shit-uation." Whether you grew up in a 'hood, a suburb, a gated community or an Ivy League campus, it will help you discover how you can begin to free yourself and our country from the "dog eat dog," hyper-individualistic, hyper-materialistic, Darwinian, survivalist, violent capitalist culture which is destroying our humanity and all life on our planet.

Yusef's journey, like Malcolm's, has been one of Transformation and Resurrection. Malcolm, also a thoughtful reader, was murdered before he was 40, leaving it to us to keep transforming our selves, as he was doing to the very end, e.g. going to Selma to tell MLK he wanted to work with him. Yusef Shakur is 36, still with us, still evolving.

At Grace's 94th birthday party, Richard introduced me to actor Danny Glover, who was the keynote speaker. Richard had given him a copy of my book. Danny was real down to earth and shared a brief intimate conversation with me. Almost two years later Danny came back to Detroit for the release of Grace's new book, *The Next American Revolution,* which Danny had written the Foreword for. I walked up to him at the event and said, "Hi". He responded by saying, "babe I loved your book, I take it with me everywhere I go." I was stunned with his response, because I didn't think he would remember my name let alone my book. The support of Grace, Detroit City of Hope and the Boggs Center allowed me to circumvent the bullshit I was encountering in the activist community that was trying to *co-opt* me. Also, they connected me with a larger community outside of Detroit, such as Professors Scott Kurashige and Stephen Ward, who both teach at the University of Michigan and have used my book in their respective classes. They have also brought me in to speak as well. Below you will find a letter from a student from the University of Michigan who came and purchased my book from my bookstore and heard me speak as well.

I knew that Yusef Shakur's "The Window 2 My Soul" was a special book before I even opened its cover. I made the decision to buy the book in person from his Urban Network Bookstore on Grand River in Detroit. I saw firsthand what an amazing place the Urban Network is: part bookstore, part cafe, and part recording studio, it stands a testament to Mr. Shakur's commitment to give back to his neighborhood, the place he once called "Zone 8". I will never forget the day I bought that book, the way the transaction was sealed with a smile and a handshake, not just the transfer of money. And I will never forget the man from whom I purchased the book: Author. I will never forget how helpful and friendly he was. And I learned his name not from a name tag or a badge, but from a conversation: he introduced himself to me, asked me what my name was, and wondered how he could help me. I have never experienced that kind of personal welcome and assistance in a store before, and I was very impressed to say the least. A few months later, when I heard Mr. Shakur speak at the University of Michigan, it all made sense when he explained that the Urban Network Café is even willing to sell its food below the market price if a potential customer cannot afford it. For Mr. Shakur, the Urban Network is not just about revenue and profits: it is about making a difference in the lives of individual people and the community at large. My chance to meet the author was just a tiny glimpse into what Mr. Shakur is doing at the Urban Network, but it was enough to make me a believer. To paraphrase his own words from his visit to U or M, Mr. Shakur really is impacting the community the way that he wishes it had impacted him. -Michael

As January 3, 2010 quickly approached, I began to reflect on the fact that I had been home 9 years after doing 9 years. So, I decided to organize a celebration event, because I believed that I had achieved two things worth recognizing. One was my transformation and the other was my active involvement in making a difference locally and nationally. The event was called "9 Years In — 9 Years Out." Every year, the mass media and certain politicians have cemented their careers on continually promoting the need to be tough on crime. This is partly due to the inordinate number of formerly incarcerated men returning back to the community only to pick up where they left off. Truth be told, the media and politicians refuse to acknowledge the fact that many of these men and women don't want to live criminal lifestyles, but are trapped by a lack of opportunities. Many of the formerly incarcerated who find themselves re-offending are desperately trying to escape the criminal lifestyle they once proudly engaged in.

There are practically no programs of substance designed to help formerly incarcerated people make a successful transition back into society. The Michigan Prison Reentry Initiative (MPRI) is setting formerly incarcerated people up for failure. As one participant once told me, "MPRI is a joke and every time I went to them for assistance, I left with none." The harsh reality is that only a handful of formerly incarcerated people are receiving help, while the rest are left to fall by the wayside.

In May of 2010, in honor of Malcolm X, a new paradigm shift was instituted and the 9 Years In — 9 Years Out: A Celebration of Redemption and Transformation was declared. Although the theme highlighted me in particular, the event celebrated the great accomplishments and good deeds of 13 other formerly incarcerated men and women who had overcome many obstacles, proving themselves as assets to their community. The event was co-sponsored by HOPE and Lakeshore Economic Coalition. Both groups were at the forefront in the City of Detroit in the fight to restore dignity and hope to formerly incarcerated men and women. All the recipients were honored with a *"Testimonial Resolution"* from Detroit City Councilman Ken Cockrel, Jr.'s office, a *"Testimonial Resolution"* from Wayne County Commissioner Bernard Parker's office, as well as a *"Special Tribute"* from State Rep Fred Durhal. Bankole Thompson, Senior Editor of the Michigan Chronicle and Hip Hop artist Khary Frazier moderated the event and Dr. Carl S. Taylor delivered the keynote address to an audience of 200 people. The honorees included Kwasi Akwamu, Tim Greer-Bey, Harold Sanders, Lindsey Wright-El, Seven the General, Derek Blackmon, Ali Morgan, Troy X, Arthur Willis, Sylvester Long, Angelita Able, Malik Shelton, Leon Jones, Demarco Hawkins and myself. The thought process behind recognizing the other individuals was that I knew I wasn't the only one out there who had redeemed their life and made a transformation. More importantly, I knew that many organizations and society as a whole play formerly incarcerated men and women against each by treating us like rats and throwing some cheese at us so that we all run for it and fight each other for a piece of cheese. That shit is sicking! Fuck that! On that day, we stood as one and recognized all of us as human beings, which has become an annual event of celebrating the redemption and transformation of formerly incarcerated men and women.

I received the prestigious "Malcolm X Award". During the acceptance I surprised my mother with the "Mothers Love Award", which honors those mothers who have stood with their children while they have done their time in the belly of the beast (prison).

Coming home from prison, I knew what I wanted to do, which was to be a difference maker in my community. That is what I was re-educated to do in prison. My activism began there along with thousands of other prisoners across this country. The prisoners I left behind expected nothing less than my coming home and being a revolutionary, because that is what I had transformed into inside of prison. The harsh reality was that there had been thousands of prisoners that had come home from prison before me with the same mission, only to result back to underdeveloped behavior. There was no blue print for me to flow, nor was there any other formerly incarcerated person for me to lean on. I had to figure it out on my own and the only thing I had to rely on was my prison experience of being an activist. I was locked in to succeed, despite facing many internal and external challenges.

Many people who have met me since I have come home seem surprised by what I have been able to accomplish over the last four years, which is clearly rooted in what I was doing in prison and long before I wrote my book. I give all credit to my father. Who I am, and what I have become, is a strong reflection of him and his influence on me through investing his time, wisdom and knowledge with me while we were both in prison. I am an extension of the type of man and leader he is. Make no mistake about it; if it wasn't for that relationship I developed with my father in prison, I wouldn't be who I am today. This past year, my father called me one day and I wasn't having a great day. Actually, I was at my breaking point from all the pressure my shoulders was carrying. I just broke down crying and told him that I was tired and that I was ready to give up from dealing with all the bullshit. He listened and responded by saying, "Son, I know it is hard for you and I wish I was out there to struggle with you, but giving up is not an option. God didn't bring this far for you to fail. Let it out, because you are carrying a lot and it will allow you to have a peace of mind and you can't do anything without a peace of mind."

Going back into prison to visit my father for the first time was a *powerful* and *emotional* experience. I was happy, sad, angry, mad, excited and every other emotion you can think of. The visit went great until it was time for us to leave. I was angry and full of rage and couldn't see myself leaving my father behind enemy lines. I was ready to go to war to liberate him from his captors. He calmed me down and conveyed to me that everything would be alright. Every visit after that wouldn't be that intense for me. I went to go see him last year for Father's Day at the prison I had paroled from. It was a surreal moment for me during the whole visit, just thinking that we were in the same visiting room that I had met my son in for the first time. It was an emotional visit for me.

My father continues to fight for his innocence after being falsely convicted of murdering another prisoner in prison. The racist courts gave him an additional 30 years on top of the 20 years he was already sentenced to for his original case which sent him to prison. As of today, my father has spent 28 consecutive years in prison. This past year (2011), I was finally able to send him some good news related to fighting for his freedom, which was that my cousin and I were able to track down the guy that lied on him and he was more than willing to sign an affidavit to indicate that he had lied. I sent the affidavit to my father and submitted it with a motion to the courts of appeals. We are hopeful that the courts will do the right thing, but when you are an oppressed man in an oppressed society, *you hope for the best, while expecting the worst.*

Visiting Oakland:
Home of the Black Panthers

Chapter 10

During the summer of 2009, I organized a community event celebrating the 2nd year anniversary of the release of my memoir with the new foreword by Dr. Carl S. Taylor. I was in my neighborhood passing out fliers at a town hall meeting inside of a church when I met City Councilman Ken Cockrel, Jr. for the first time. We talked briefly and I gave him one of the fliers for my event. He told me that he would be attending, but I really didn't put too much stock into it since I had supported Freeman Hendrix for Mayor. On the day of the election, Hendrix invited me to the Mildred Gaddis radio show to help him promote. It was my first time meeting Mildred Gaddis and appearing on her show, but she and her listeners were impressed with my story. After the votes were tallied up, Hendrix hadn't received enough to win the election so he disappeared like most politicians do after they lose. They all *proclaim* how much they want to make a difference, but they fail to disclose to the voters that it is only predicated upon them winning the election. If they don't win, we never hear from them unless they decide to run again. So, my attitude with Ken Cockrel, Jr. was that, "I will believe it when I see it!"

When my event arrived, I was pleasantly surprised to see Councilman Cockrel there with his oldest son. He had not only made good on his word, but he had bought a book from me for his son. The event was a huge success and a few days later I received a phone call from my mama telling me that City Councilman Ken Cockrel, Jr. had dropped something off for me. When I got there and opened up my package, it was a *"Testimonial of Resolution"* for the second edition of my book. He had also left a message for me to call him so, I was speechless. I called his office and was advised that he wanted to have a meeting with me and I agreed. During the meeting he asked how he could be more supportive of my efforts, because being a politician didn't allow him to be on the ground level like I was. I hesitated to respond to his question, because asking for help had never been a strong suit of mine. I then responded by asking for support with my annual back to school supply drive. He agreed and assigned his staff member Coit Ford III, who had been in the room documenting the meeting, as the point person who would work with me. Ken Cockrel, Jr. would later describe me like this in an interview on 101.9FM:

What he does, he does really on a shoestring budget, but never the less he's been able to have a very important impact. He's not out here running a foundation that has a corner office in some high rise building with a couple of secretaries and lots of computers and cell phones and lots of technology...He's doing what he does in a very grassroots, simple way and yet he is still having a very important impact and the way in which he does things is very significant as well, because he still very much has a finger on the pulse of the streets.

That year, City Councilman Cockrel's office became an official sponsor of the annual back to school supply drive. I was also able to get Flip the Script to co-sponsor the event, because of my relationship with Keith Bennett who was one the first people to buy a bulk of my books for his Flip the Script program. Over the last three years, City Councilman Cockrel's office with Coit Ford, III being the point person, has raised close to $10,000 in support of the back to school supply drive. Because of their support, the second year we were able to give away close to 150 backpacks, 250 backpacks the following year and 500 backpacks the next year, along with free food, games, live entertainment and many giveaways each year as well.

What impressed me most about Ken Cockrel, Jr. was that he never used his support of the annual back to school supply drive to openly promote himself like most politicians would have. He never showed up with the media for *photo-opts* and each year he came with one of his children. It was a pure *labor of love* for him with the end goal of impacting Detroiters in a real meaningful way. Over the years we have developed a close friendship, but unfortunately, he gets a bad rap because he lives in the *shadow* of who his dad was. Although he has carved his own path as one of the very few standup politicians as a member of Detroit's City Council, his father Ken Cockrel, Sr. is a legendary Detroit activist who as a lawyer fought against racial injustice in the court room and in the streets. Ken Cockrel, Jr. has my unconditional support, because he too has fought for Detroiters in a very principled way.

One day I received a phone call from Richard Feldman informing me that the Boggs Center was co-sponsoring a bus trip to Greensboro, North Carolina to attend a conference in remembrance of the 30 year anniversary of the "Greensboro Massacre". Needless to say, I jumped at the opportunity!

At the time of the trip to Greensboro, North Carolina I was a 36 year old Black man in amerikkka who had never been *down south*. I felt like a little boy taking a trip to visit relatives. Unfortunately, for many Black males in urban amerikkka the ritual of taking a trip *down south* to visit relatives has been replaced with the ritual of taking a trip *up north* to modern day slave camps *aka* prisons. This harsh reality is a by-product of the social, political, educational, cultural, spiritual and economic deterioration that is at the root of manufacturing human decay in urban amerikkka.

During the 12 hour drive from Detroit to Greensboro, I felt so relaxed and relieved. It was the first time in a long time that I wasn't anticipating a phone call, rushing to get to a meeting, only to leave that meeting to rush to another meeting, or doing everything for everybody else while finding no time in the day for myself. During the drive from Detroit to Greensboro, the eight of us immediately began to bond. This made my decision to take the trip that much more rewarding. I knew that being afforded an opportunity to build relationships with the people I was on the trip with would prove invaluable. When we finally arrived at our living quarters, my comrads and I all dispersed to our sleeping areas. We were all excited to be in Greensboro and eagerly anticipated attending the conference the following day. The next morning the Detroit collective arrived early at the conference with a glow as bright as the sun.

Nelson Johnson was the first person we saw as we entered the conference and he instantly recognized Bill Wylie-Kellerman, a Detroit pastor who was with us on the trip. Nelson shared with us that the people of Greensboro had recently been dealt a severe blow with the defeat of their Mayor at the time and certain City Council members. He felt that it was a direct result of their political support of the efforts to keep the memory of the 1979 massacre alive. Even though he was visibly disturbed by the defeat, you could just sense that it would not stop him from continuing to *fight the good fight*. After hearing this news, my mind

133

began to think about the elections in Detroit, specifically regarding my displeasure with Dave Bing who is now the current Mayor. Not only because I had made an attempt to give him one of my books when I met him, only to have it handed back to me after being coldly told that he didn't have time to read such a book, but I knew that if he was elected, he would be more concerned about *corporate Detroit* than *downtrodden Detroit.* I also thought about how certain people had been *hoodwinked* and *bamboozled* into electing City Council members because of name recognition, instead of individuals who had the work experience of being effective in serving the people of Detroit. I carefully listened to Nelson as he briefly stressed the importance of establishing and cultivating relationships with certain City officials who express a desire to go beyond their call of duty, by being servants of the people. It was important for me to hear this and examine what he was saying because of the attention I was attracting from certain City officials, as an actively involved community leader in Detroit.

During the first day of the conference, we watched a documentary which highlighted the killings by the Klan members and showed how the Greensboro police arrived afterwards only to arrest those who had survived the bloody massacre. Even though I knew what I was watching was real, my mind could not comprehend that innocent people had been *openly murdered.* I instantly began to think back to Detroit and reflect on the murder of Imam Luqman Ameen Abdullah, who had been shot over 18 times by the FBI. Connecting the past to the present boldly reminded me of the bloody acts of the FBI's COINTELPRO, which included murdering FREEDOM FIGHTERS as well as FALSELY incarcerating them. The only crime that these heroes committed was that they were REVOLUTIONARIES committed to REVOLUTION on amerikkkan soil. The relevance of the past with the present was so clear; *that those in power will never relinquish their power without a fight and that they are willing to fight till the death.*

When the documentary ended, those who had survived the massacre were asked to give their accounts of that bloody day. Each one of them gave a vivid account of November 3, 1979 that left us all speechless. When Paul Bermanzohn spoke, his testimony was not only as a survivor of a massacre, but as a freedom fighter who emphasized that we must continue to resist oppression *by any means!* He had survived gunshot wounds which left him partially paralyzed on one side of his

134

body and he was still spirited and teaching liberation! This was so inspiring to me and it renewed my commitment to the struggle in an immeasurable way. Not only did I feel like he was passing his torch, but I felt like he was speaking directly to me saying, *"I will still struggle and fight with you"*. I felt connected to him and the struggle and more importantly, I felt the obligation to continue the struggle. I was so deeply moved by what Paul had shared that I gave him a signed copy of my *Memoir* to show the appreciation, love and respect I had developed for him.

The struggle for social justice must be continued, but it can only be continued if it is passed down from generation to generation. This way, the lessons of past generations will be taught effectively. When the past is repeated without proper knowledge of history, many are left to find their own way through the maze of confusion and oppression. Although I am well read on the protracted struggle in amerikkka, having the ability to absorb actual history has had a profound impact on me, by re-enforcing everything I had already read. Reading from a book is fine, but there is nothing like receiving firsthand knowledge from someone who has lived it and is willing to share their wisdom. That is crucial to the transformational struggle that is currently taking place, because it gives transformational education through examples we can learn from. More importantly, as the great George Jackson wrote: *I refuse to allow future generations to curse me, as I curse those before me.* It is imperative that the elder generation engage the younger generation in cultivating the passing of the *torch*. I was glad to see in Greensboro that this was taking place.

After an intense period of sharing potent information throughout the conference, we finally broke to go eat dinner before the next two events. The first of which would be a march with college students to a museum to view another movie about the Greensboro massacre. When we departed from the church to go the restaurant to eat, everybody jumped into different cars and I found myself riding with Nelson. I immediately began asking him questions in order to pick his brain and learn as much as I could in that short period of time. After I could not think of anymore questions for him, he began to ask me some so, I briefly shared my journey with him. He responded by saying that he wished he had read my book before I came because Bill had sent a copy of it to him. I was so honored to spend that brief time with Nelson, because he was a down to earth type of person that related to me in a way which allowed me to connect with him. I wanted to be a part of what he was doing, because his leadership style was similar to that of Earl Wheeler, Cicero Love and General Baker. What all these men have in common to me is a *valley type-of-leadership* which is needed in rebuilding our communities and reclaiming our families. Unfortunately, what we have more of is a *mountain type-of-leadership* that keeps us confused and lacking an overstanding of our shit-uation.

Once we were done eating, we departed for the museum to watch the movie. When we arrived, the theater was packed with college students. One thing that stood out to me about the movie was the part which highlighted survivors of the massacre at a beach having fun together. Out of their ordeal, they were able to cultivate family ties with each other which provided them with the necessary strength, support and love to continue to live despite what they had been through. The unfortunate circumstances of being involved in such a historic tragedy had forged a bond which would allow them and their families to heal together. During the movie, I noticed a Latino brother enter the theater. I immediately realized it was Jorge Cornell/King J the leader of the Almighty Latin Kings and Queens Nation whom I was I selected to do a workshop with the next day. I got up and introduced myself to him and we talked briefly. He shared with me his disappointment in not winning a seat in the City Council race among other things and an instant bond between the two of us was born.

By the time we got back to our living quarters that evening, I was exhausted because I had received so much information throughout the day. So, I immediately went to bed to digest it. When morning arrived, we followed our same routine of leaving early so that we could arrive early. When we got there, Bill was approached by one of the organizers. After speaking with her, he came over to me and asked if I would mind filling in for King J as one of the presenters during the "Healing Circle", because they were unsure if he would make it. I had thought the day before was real intense at the conference, but being a part of the "Healing Circle" took it to another level. Listening to the relatives of those who had been murdered and survived the massacre hit an emotional chord in all of us, which put things in a human perspective. It became clear that as human beings we take a lot for granted. As things progressed during the "Healing Circle", King J arrived to share his story, which I was excited to hear. He shared with us that he felt the need to start the Almighty Latin Kings and Queens Nation in Greensboro as a direct result of the police's harassment of Latinos. As a result of his community organizing in politicizing Latino youth, he became *public enemy number 1* and had been charged over 20 times with trumped-up charges, which were either dismissed or he was found not guilty of them. He then shared with us that an attempt on his life had been made, which he believed was by the Greensboro police. Fortunately, he was not left on an island by himself to face the harassment by the police. Nelson, along with other pastors and community leaders wrapped their arms around him and stood with him demanding justice and that the harassment be stopped. I believe it was sincere support, because they overstood the history of the Greensboro police from the lessons they had learned from 1979. I shared with King J that I wished I could get the type of support from religious and community leaders in Detroit like he had in Greensboro.

In Detroit there is an abundance of *elitism leadership* that has suffocated this City to its death bed. It is a reflection of certain religious leaders, activists, businesses, non-profits, conscious community and political leaders which only operate in their little circle(s) and if you are not part of one of these circles, you find yourself on the outside looking in. The only time you are invited to be a part of one of these *elite circles* is if they see that they can benefit from you. Despite this reactionary leadership and having *TEFLON SKIN,* I have been able to find my way as one the most energetic leaders to emerge in Detroit in a long time.

A close comrad of mine shared with me a biblical scripture, "*a prophet is not honored in his own home.*" Those few words have stuck with me as I have traveled to cities outside of Detroit. The people in those cities have showered me with so much love that I have began to question whether is it worth putting up with all the bullshit in Detroit. When I am at those low points in my life, I begin to reflect on all the people in Detroit who are depending on me and have found some type of hope, inspiration and dignity in the things that I am doing on a grassroots/ground zero level. It is then that I find the strength to continue to struggle at home.

The unique thing about attending the conference in Greensboro was the atmosphere. I was somewhere where I didn't have to prove

137

anything to anybody and they accepted me as if I was a family member. When I was asked to participate in the Healing Circle, I felt so honored. Initially, there wasn't enough time for me to share my story during the Healing Circle, but I was cool with that because again, I was just honored to be there. However, because of the anticipation of people wanting to hear my story, organizers altered the conference after lunch and we all came back together for the Healing Circle so that I could share my story. That was one of the most powerful experiences in my young life and it re-enforced in my mind the type of leadership that is necessary to lead the people, which is one that has to be flexible, innovative, honest and has its finger on the pulse of the people.

We then attended a dinner event with the pastors to discuss the dynamics of the U.S. Social Forum, which was to be held in Detroit in June of 2010. The conversation centered on people in Greensboro attending the forum and many of the pastors presented legitimate questions and concerns about it. However, the most powerful thing that was said during the dinner meeting was when one of the pastors said, "If Nelson said it is important for us to be there, then we will be there." During the whole time we were in Greensboro, it was clear that Nelson was the leader of the event. However, he never felt the need to be the center of attention. His unique leadership style is refreshing, because it encourages others to be leaders right beside him. He engages people in a way that empowers them to realize their own potential. It reminded me of when I met my father, Professor Carl S. Taylor, Linda Evens, Arthur "Tha" League, Dorsey Nunn, Tom Hardiman, William Copeland, Charles Simmons, Malik Yakini, Ron Scott and Richard Feldman. They immediately embraced me and found time in their busy lives to help nurture and guide me with wisdom and knowledge to further grow as a leader. That is crucial in the 21st century, if we are to make sanity out of the insane shit-uation we find ourselves in. Practical leadership is necessary and more importantly needed in order to cultivate new leaders to engage the people where they are and in order to teach them how to move to where they need to be. This type of leadership will only come when a true pro-people orientation is instituted. Being in Greensboro reaffirmed in me that a new world is possible, that a new world is happening and that I play a crucial role in its development.

When we got back from Greensboro, North Carolina the talk in Detroit was about the U.S. Social Forum and getting ready for it, but I was still trying to wrap my mind around it and what it meant for Detroiters. The U.S. Social Forum is a gathering in the United States of amerikkka of social activists from around the world. The goal is to unite likeminded people who are dedicated to social justice. The U.S. Social Forum grew out of the World Social Forum and the first one was held in Atlanta in 2007.

A meeting was held at the Boggs Center, where organizers from the community based organization "Project South" were invited to share their experiences in helping to organize the first U.S. Social Forum in Atlanta. During the meeting, I asked a lot of questions and certain Detroit organizers of the U.S. Social Forum felt like I was sabotaging their meeting. After the meeting Emery Lumumba of "Project South" conveyed to me that I had asked some great questions, because the questions I asked were the same questions they asked while organizing the U.S. Social Forum in Atlanta.

William Copeland, a strong Detroit activist reached out to me and brought me on board as part of the community outreach team about two months before the U.S. Social Forum was brought here to Detroit. Over 20,000 activists from around the world came to participate. Attending and speaking at the U.S. Social Forum was one of the most defining moments in my young life. It was the first time since my gang banging days that I felt at home. I met great people who were sharing priceless information. The event impacted me the same way my father did while we were both in prison, an interaction which initiated my transformation from a Zone 8 thug to a freedom fighter. This experience was valuable to me, because it re-enforced the importance of the work that I am doing here in Detroit, introduced me to people across the country, gave me a sense of being part of a movement beyond Detroit and challenged me to reflect upon and to be a reflection of my work.

This historical gathering granted me the wonderful opportunity to meet my extended family: All of Us or None. When I was at the U.S. Social Forum, Dorsey Nunn and Arthur "Tha" League approached me. Both were members of All of Us or None and conveyed to me that everybody that they talked to about doing work on behalf of formerly incarcerated people, mentioned my name. They didn't hesitate to search me out and when they approached me I felt honored to be enlisted to do work on behalf of formerly incarcerated people as a member of All of Us or None.

It was a contingent of members of All of Us or None that had come to Detroit and I had the great pleasure of meeting them all, including long standing activist and former political prisoner Linda Evans. She began her organizing in 1965 at Michigan State University as a member of the "Students for a Democratic Society (SDS)". She was sentenced in 1987 to 40 years in prison for using false identification to buy firearms and harboring a fugitive in the 1981 Brinks armored truck robbery. On January 20, 2001 former President Bill Clinton commuted her sentence of 40 years and she only served 16 years of her sentence. We hit it off immediately and she adopted me as her little brother and as my mentor. Linda is one of the most beautiful human beings I have ever met.

All of Us or None is a national organizing initiative started by formerly incarcerated people to fight against discrimination faced after release and to fight for the human rights of prisoners. We are determined to win full restoration of our civil and human rights after release from prison. Our goal is to build political power in the communities most affected by mass incarceration and the growth of the Prison Industrial Complex. The emergence of All of Us or None is a concrete manifestation of the people most affected by an issue, building a movement to combat it. Because the membership of All of Us or None is predominantly people of color, our emergence as a leading organization in the white-dominated criminal justice/anti-prison movement has a concrete impact on this movement. We're committed to organizing formerly-incarcerated people to build a movement across the nation, by working in coalition with other community groups and organizing campaigns, such as Ban the Box which we initiated over 10 years ago and has taken root in communities in different states and across the nation.

Months had passed since meeting Dorsey and Tha at the U.S. Social Forum. However, Tha stayed in contact with me afterwards and mentioned that he was interested in flying me out to the Bay area. Soon after, I received a phone call from Tha asking if I was free to fly out to the Bay in November and I said yes. He then asked me if there was a certain day that I had to be back and I told him that I was free to stay as long as possible. Although I was excited about flying out to the Bay area for the first time, I had no clue what my experience would be like and I actually began to get cold feet leading up to my trip. I was nervous, because I had never spent more than a weekend away from Detroit besides my nine years of incarceration. Luckily, I didn't let my cold feet stop me from spending 20 days in the place that gave birth to the Black Panther Party.

Once I arrived in the Bay, Tha introduced me to Sundiata (Willie Tate) and David Johnson, who were both members of the San Quentin Six and comrads of George Jackson. I also met Harold Taylor and the Freeman brothers, who were all members of the L.A. chapter of the BPP and served under the leadership of Bunchy Carter. Never in my lifetime did I think that I would meet comrads of George Jackson and Bunchy Carter. I conveyed to them how much I admired and respected them. They conveyed to me how much they admired and respected me as well. That Bay area trip wouldn't have been possible without my comrad Tha and I am forever grateful to him for that. Tha has an over 40-year history as a community activist involved in social and criminal justice work. In the 70's & 80's, during a time of political unrest, Tha was an active member of the Black Panther Party. His political beliefs and actions resulted in his serving seven years in the California State Prison system. Tha is a founding member of *Timers* and *All of Us or None*, community led organizations of formerly-incarcerated individuals committed to empowering people in communities most affected by the Prison Industrial Complex. Also, during my trip, Tha introduced me to his long standing comrad "L-Man". L-Man was a bright and intelligent brother that immediately took to me and never hesitated during my trip and afterwards to invest and share his wisdom, knowledge and history with me in strengthening my development of being a revolutionary.

While Tha, L-Man and I were driving through the Bay, the word "chick" came out of my mouth. Tha pulled the car over; they both looked back at me and conveyed to me that my language was not conducive to describing women. I openly accepted their criticism of me even though I meant no harm by it. However, the fact remained that my language displayed a sexist tone. Through that experience from my comrads they were reinforcing that we can't have true equality, freedom, justice and liberation if the only roles we provide for women are as sex objects, note takers, cooks, babysitters and maids, etc. These actions are nothing but an extension of oppression.

One of the great things about being around many of the seasoned activists was that I was able to learn firsthand from them. Any question I could think of, they had an answer because they all had lived what I desired to be, a *revolutionary* and none of them hesitated to teach me and correct me. I valued every minute I was with them and cherish the many lessons they shared with me.

During my incarceration, I had the great pleasure of learning a lot from reading "Seize the Time", "Blood in My Eye", "This Side of Glory", "Taste of Power", "Soledad Brother" and many other books about the Black Panther Party and our struggles. Being out there in the Bay granted me the opportunity to learn *firsthand* so much more from brothers and sisters who were there to help contribute to writing that part of history. Unfortunately, some were names and faces that may never appear in a book. David Hilliard, the former Chief of Staff of the BPP took me out to lunch and had conveyed to me that, "the same conditions that gave birth to the BPP in Oakland in 1966 exist in Detroit". I totally agreed with him and those conditions he talked about are what gave birth to my community organizing of *restoring the neighbor back to the 'hood.*

My trip blessed me with the chance to meet many of my heroes and sheroes as well as pay homage to one of our fallen souljahs "Marilyn Buck" who is considered, as stated by comrads, THE JOHN BROWN OF OUR TIME for her actions and others in the liberation of Assata Shakur from prison. I also had the great honor of meeting legendary activist, Angela Davis. They all embraced me and more importantly, were willing to share the many lessons that they have learned from being on the frontlines as well as survivors of the vicious attack from COINTELPRO. Just being in the Bay area is *inspiring* in itself. It is a place that has a rich history of protracted struggle and a diverse culture.

142

The people that I connected with while I was there have embraced me as a son, brother and a comrad!

While out there, I had the great opportunity of being a spectator at a lot of the events and rallies. I enjoyed myself because it had been a long time since I had been afforded an opportunity to just be a spectator. As a spectator, I had the chance to do some *window shopping* where I was able to evaluate every aspect of what it means to be a community organizer. Words such as precision, efficiency, effectiveness and others come to mind, which need to be attached to the end result of achieving our goals. We can't continue to organize from an emotional standpoint. That standpoint will never sustain our work as community organizers and will continue to leave us organizing in circles. We also cannot be insensitive to the needs of the community. If we organize the community around their needs, they will begin to take their destiny into their own hands. As my comrad Harold shared with me one day while I was out there, "having principles and discipline is our greatest asset as community organizers." Being armed with *discipline of thought* is necessary to enhance our people skills because without people skills, we will be poor community organizers!

The time that I spent in the Bay and the two days I spent in L.A. were life-changing experiences. My *passion* has grown deeper, my *vision* is clearer, my *dedication* is stronger and I *embrace* my role as a leader more than ever! Love inspires all things that are positive, because when we experience genuine love, it inspires us to love ourselves and others genuinely. The love my elder comrad Tha has shown me is the type of love that inspires a person to reach their full potential as a human being! The time out there was like going off to school and finally being with teachers that overstood my potential and were willing to help me develop it. The significant thing that I learned (or should I say re-learned), was the importance of sacrifice as well as how we must remove ourselves from *personality worshipping,* if we are to embark upon the journey of changing our communities as a whole. More importantly, this task cannot be achieved without the leadership of women!

I have heard the word *COMRAD* used a lot. However, it wasn't until going out to the Bay and L.A. and being around the elder brothers & sisters (*both white and Black*) that I have seen the meaning demonstrated unconditionally. The trust that they have is unbreakable

143

and it is rooted in the struggle of overcoming all types of oppression. More significantly, the love they have for one another is stronger than anything *materialistic*. They are critical of each other with the sole purpose of challenging their comrads to succeed. The political line that governs them daily is that *ALL CONTRADICTIONS ARE NOT ANTAGONISTIC*. Even as they embrace the new generation of community activists, they just have one question, "What are your programs?" Programs are what allow us to win the hearts and minds of the people. When we are being efficient, precise and effective through our programs to meet and serve their needs, it empowers them to take their destiny into their own hands! *The center of our work starts with winning the hearts and minds of the people!*

Even though it is real tempting to want to stay out in the Bay, because I believe I would strive even harder, in the back of my mind I would be thinking I left a job unfinished back in Detroit. The Bay is like my second home, but I must remain in my first home until I finish my job. The most significant thing that transpired when I was out there was that I finally discovered what I desired to be, which is a *TRUE REVOLUTIONARY!*

Before I left the Bay, I was able to hold a book discussion at two different legendary places. One was at the "Black Dot" located in West Oakland and the other was at "Marcus Bookstore" in San Francisco, the first Black bookstore in amerikkka. I was honored to hold events at such historical places and I returned to Detroit more than ready to embrace my role as a leader.

Me, Prostell & his son doing a community clean up on the Eastside of Detroit.

Me & Khary receiving the Silent Hero Awards. We have work together on numerous community projects to better Detroit.

145

Reggie Reg Davis & myself. Through his Cease Fire organization
he brought me on board to tour Detroit Public Schools to share my story.

Me with Latonya Hardiman receiving the Local Hero Award from Bank
of America. The Hardiman family has been big supporters of mine.

Me receiving the Leaders, Legends & Luminaries Award from Avinash Rachmale & Tom Hardiman.

Me standing with a group of youth who graduated from a 20 week youth program I facilitated. We have over 200 people come to support them for their graduation.

Me & Dr Carl S. Taylor with youth from Detroit in the area where
the 1967 rebellion began.

Me & Congressman Conyers in my
Bookstore.

Me, City Councilman Cockrel Jr
& his son standing together in Z8ne.

Me with City Councilmen's Spivey & Tate at my 9yr celebration.

Me with Judge Mathis.

Me & radio personality John Mason.

Me standing with youth from Z8ne reading my book.

Me speaking at the 2nd U.S. Social Forum in Detroit.

Me & Ron Scott (former BPP) leading a march in Detroit down west 7 Mile.

Me in North Carolina with Nelson Johnson & his wife.

Me with my All of Us or None family from the Bay Area in Detroit.

Tha (former BPP), myself & Sunidata in the Bay Area out for lunch.

Me & Angela Davis.   Me & Bobby Seal (former BPP).

Me & David Hillard (former BPP). Me & Big Man (former BPP).

David Johnson, myself & Sundiata (bothe were comrads of George Jackson & members of the San Quentin Six.)

Me & the Freeman brothers (former BPP).   Me & Erica Huggins (former BPP).

Me & Harold Taylor (former BPP).   Me & Malik Rahim (former BPP).

Me & Linda Evans (former political prisoner).

Me & Manuel in Alabama at the Formerly Incarcerated &
Convicted Peoples gathering...Black & Brown unity is a must.

Me in Musegon with Dr. Jackson.   Me & Marsha in Mt. Pleasant.

Me with a group of students up north in Michigan I spoke too.

Me with a group of high school students in Mt. Pleasant I spoke too.

A photo of me speaking at Central Michigan University where I spoke to an audience of 300 students.

Me standing with a group of honor students at CMU I spoke too.

Me & Shaka standing with a group of students in Wisconsin we spoke too.

Me speaking at the
Heal Detroit gathering.

Me & Jeff Edison a member of the National Black
Lawyers at a community event.

Me & my comrad 7 the General.

160

Detroit standing in solidarity with the Georgia prison strike.

Amber, myself & Honeycomb.

A brother reading my book in Muskegon at a park.

Poet Khary Turner reading my book for the 2nd yr anniversary of releasing it.

Me & Squeak former gang enemies Standing in Z8ne as brothers.

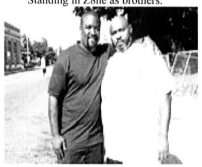

Me speaking at the Urban Network.

162

Me with Danny Glovery & him telling me how much he loved my book.

Shaka & I with Dr. Cornel West in Wisconsin at a conference we spoke at.

Me & my homie Li Li playing chess in Z8ne.

Me & Kobie playing chess at the Urban Network.

DeAngelo & Kobie having fun in a swimming pool at my mom's house.

Me & Chief of Police Ralph Godbee embrace at my 10 yr celebration.

Me & mom's at my 9 yr celebration after I gave her an award.

Me at the "State of the Neighborhood Address" I did in Z8ne.

Me & Joanna who has been my rock.

Me on Detroit Fox 2 "Let It Rip". I was nervous & excited about being on the show.

Dear Zone 8:
Restoring the Neighbor back to the 'Hood

Chapter 11

I attribute the success I've obtained to my hard work and dedication as well as my loyalty to where I came from. It was always my goal to return back to my neighborhood Zone 8 and firmly plant my feet in the soil of the place I once took pride in destroying. I was devoted to rebuilding it. I was receiving support from a lot of people who had no knowledge of my neighborhood and were trying to entice me to branch out into other areas as a base, but I wasn't having it! Although I knew the challenges I would face by going back to Zone 8 would be daunting, I refused to turn my back on them like everyone else did. I was committed to my neighborhood for better or for worse and I was armed with the thought process that if I couldn't use my new found social prestige to improve the quality of life in Zone 8, *I wasn't nothing but another nigga being pimped.* I was motivated to serve my community the way I wished that someone had served it when I was young, by providing an example of being an educated and positive Black man. More importantly, I was doing it for all of my homies who are locked up, died young or was drug addicts and was never given a fair opportunity to show the world their potential as human beings. If they had been provided with the right *resources*, many of them could have been a judge, lawyer, doctor and etc.

We call our neighborhood Zone 8 because of the zip code 48208. It is also reported that the police are the ones who named it that back in the late 60s as a way to identify our neighborhood. That name stuck with us and was something we all took pride in. Before Black people moved into Zone 8, it was known as Northwest Goldberg and was populated by white Jews who decided to move out once Black people started to move in. Our Black neighborhood at one time mirrored any white neighborhood in the state of Michigan. It was a community rich in love, culture, vibrant businesses and people who cared about each other. The people who lived in my neighborhood demanded the best and provided the best for their children and their neighbors. At some point, this could be said about all Black neighborhoods in the City of Detroit.

After 1967, Detroit changed dramatically for Black people. That is the year that ushered in what is considered the worst race riot in amerikkkan history. When you talk to most Detroiters about 1967, they make sure to clarify that it wasn't a race riot, it was a *rebellion*. The rebellion erupted a few blocks from my neighborhood on 12th and Clairmount after the police raided an after-hour joint known then as a "blind pig". The confrontation between the police and members of the community led to a five day rebellion. During those five days, Detroit was set ablaze. People were fighting to expose the racial injustice that was occurring on the ground level. Black bodies were being raped and beaten daily by the racist police so the people in the community became an *urban army* fighting them tooth and nail for Black justice. Thousands of national guards and other police were called in to detain the *angry niggers* and it was an all out war between both sides. Unfortunately, the Black Detroiters who were fighting on the ground level and from rooftops were eventually outnumbered and outgunned. When the smoked cleared, it is reported that 43 people were killed (majority Black), 467 were injured (majority Black), 7,231 (6,528 adults and 703 juveniles) arrests were made (majority Black) 2,509 stores were looted or burned, over 380 families lost their homes and over 400 buildings had to be demolished (majority Black). The estimated financial loss of the 1967 riot was between $40 to $80 million dollars.

It has also been documented that during the 1967 rebellion, the racist Detroit police or racist national guards had killed three Black men and two white women and several other Black men were brutally beaten almost to death at the "Algiers Motel." The Racist police/national guards were supposedly following up on a tip that a reported gunman, who was fighting against the racist police invasion of Detroit, was hanging out there. The racist police/national guards were never charged in the brutal murdering of the three Black men or the brutal beating of the others. The once Algiers Motel stood at the corner of Woodard Ave and Virginia Park and it was demolished with the accounts of that bloody day. This incident of blatant racist police brutality like many others across amerikkka, is as part of the culture of amerikkka as an apple pie!

Dr. Carl S. Taylor who grew up right smack in the middle of the area where the rebellion erupted describes Detroit as he knew it before 1967 and what Detroit became after 1967:

169

An accounting of strong role models out of my neighborhood is
impressive. There were public servants, educators, clergy, skilled
artisans, professional athletes, professional entertainers, doctors,
lawyers and the list goes on. Not dope dealers, murderers, or rapists.
That was before the riot of 1967, and then it seemed that someone just
cast darkness over the city. The riot of 1967 hurled the neighborhoods
into a darkness that no longer loved or cared about its people. As if it
was Biblical, like a curse of some sort, Detroit was invaded by heroin.
The once proud city of numerous block clubs fell short, or just
disappeared. Children became dangerous or in danger. Heroin, sadly,
was the first assault on Detroit. Families seemed to just morph into
something totally different from all the past tradition of God-fearing
communities. Whites fled, leaving behind pockets of abandoned
businesses, homes, and people. Resentment rose, hate spread with ghetto
horror stories running amok. Police units continued a campaign of
search and destroy tactics that sparked the original insurrection during
the hot July of 1967. That seemed to be the death of the city I knew, the
neighborhood that raised me and my younger brother Virgil.

The Detroit Dr. Carl S. Taylor described in the latter part of his
passage is the one that I grew up in. I can remember vividly, going
outside to play as a little boy and watching the guys in the neighborhood
holding down the corners, gas stations and neighborhood blocks selling
dope and gang banging as if they had a *license* to do it. Nobody
challenged them. Their behavior became the norm for those of us looking
at their every move. Watching them was like going to class and learning
firsthand how to become a *social monster/renegade* hell bent on
destroying the community through the underdeveloped behavior of
selling dope and gang banging.

Unfortunately, this behavior is evident now more than ever in
my neighborhood. It is a direct result of the young people being exposed
to underdeveloped images 90% of the time. This shapes their
impressionable minds to accept the streets as a way of life, which is a
death-style they have embraced and will pass on to their children,
because unfortunately, urban households and schools have become
breeding grounds for thugs and gangstas/underdeveloped behavior.

Today, when you walk through my neighborhood Zone 8, you
see blight, despair, degradation, decay, hopelessness and helplessness. I

overstand that this is a direct result of resources being cut off to neighborhoods like Zone 8. They have dried up like a lake desperately in need of water in order to thrive. Because of a lack of resources and support, people have begun to turn on each other as a means to get over (survive), which promotes the 'hood mentalities which are a reflection of a death-style that has become a way of life for many people. The young people who are being raised in this savage state begin to adopt this mindset and have no connection to anything but money, mack and murder with the end result being self-destruction.

When speaking to different audiences across the country, I often tell the story of when my mother made me a ward of the state at the age of 15. I tell that story; because it is still *relevant* today from the many mothers I talk too, who are raising their sons in the concrete jungles of urban amerikkka. At the time my mother made the decision, I couldn't comprehend the internal battle she had to wrestle with. I didn't recognize that her goal was to save me from myself. She had seen something that my Zone 8 mentality wouldn't allow me to see, which was that I was traveling the road of possibly dying or going to prison. She decided that neither was going to happen on her watch and she made a decision that only a parent would make. My mother had me locked up, not because she wanted to, but because that was the only option she had to save her son from the streets. There was no pastor, city councilman/woman, social program or recreation center she could call or take me to.

Unfortunately, that is still the same shit-uation today for many parents across this country. My mother's decision did me a world of good, because when I came home from being incarcerated, I was on the right track and even getting good grades in school. One of my teachers noticed me and asked me about going to college and I responded by telling him that I would love to go to college. So, he said he would help me. When I went home that night and reflected on our conversation it scared the living hell out of me! I had no fucking clue what college was and honestly never saw myself attending college. The irony in my lack of familiarity with college is that the famous Wayne State University "WSU" was right behind my neighborhood and I had rode my bike by it hundreds of times. Plus, WSU never made a pipeline to my neighborhood by recruiting the youth to go there. Today, all of the new development that WSU is doing in the white community "Mid-Town" is shining an even brighter light on the lack of empathy WSU administration has for the surrounding neighborhoods nearby, which are still severely neglected. Then you have Henry Ford Hospital that has initiated a *gentrification* process in my neighborhood of Zone 8 by buying up all the property with no real intent to start from the bottom to help develop it. Both Henry Ford Hospital and WSU has set on the sideline for years watching the decay of my neighborhood Zone 8 and did nothing!!!

So, when the opportunity presented itself for me to lease a store front in Zone 8, I began to explore every avenue possible. I asked the guys I was associating with at the time, their opinion of the building I was considering leasing. I saw the fear in their eyes and they shared with me why I shouldn't open a business in such an area. If I had followed conventional wisdom, I would have listened to them, but since I am an unconventional person, I brushed their doubt off of my shoulders and locked myself into opening a bookstore in my neighborhood. It was perfect after being denied the opportunity to shelf my book at several bookstores. My attitude was, "fuck it I will open up my own bookstore." I decided to call it "Urban Network" and it would be a multi-purpose store that sold books, Afrikan art, provided a meeting place for community discussions, a recording studio and we would host a weekly rap battle.

I talked my childhood friend "Black John" and two guys I was incarcerated with, Shabazz and Greer-Bey into becoming my partners. The only thing that was initially working for us was our weekly rap battles, because we were packing our place out for it. However, people weren't buying any of our products so, for the most part, we didn't make a profit our first two years. Shabazz ended up pulling out, because he lost his job and my homie Black John ended up going back to prison for a gun case. My comrad Kwasi ended up joining the team. He has been a friend, comrad and big brother to me ever since we met back in prison in 1994 via letters, helping me further develop myself into who I am today. Besides my parents, I have to credit my comrads Kwasi and Greer-Bey who also helped shape me to be the activist, organizer and leader that I am today, because of the type of leaders, organizers and activist that they are.

Having the bookstore provided me with a base operation for the activism and organizing I was doing. Also, it provided a place for the people in the neighborhood to continue to follow and see concrete evidence of what I was doing. Most people were proud of me, because I was a homeboy from the neighborhood doing something none of them ever expected, *including myself*. They saw that I didn't use dope money or any other illegal means to publish my book or run my business so, this solidified my credibility as a transformed man. This afforded them an opportunity to witness firsthand all the hard work and dedication I invested into being in the position I was in. It was the first time many of them had ever seen anything like that and it provided the older people with something they hadn't seen in a long time.

Of course, there were the few who doubted me and made comments behind my back. However, that didn't hinder my passion to be a positive example for my community, because I firmly believed that a person without passion is like a car without gas, you ain't going nowhere! One of the craziest things some guys said behind my back was that I was *snitching* in my book, because I wrote it about the neighborhood. This was insane because everybody knew that I had gone to prison and served 9 years for a crime I DID NOT commit! I had not taken the stand against anybody, but had witnessed tons of shit go down that I never talked about. I brushed it off since none of them would come to my face and make their comments. Plus, I overstood their behavior clearly. I was going against the grain and challenging the *subculture of the streets* and that wasn't acceptable, because many of them only saw themselves as dope sellers, people who hang on the corners talking shit, packing guns and just waiting on the next stick-up job. Everything balanced out when some of my O.G. homies expressed that they respected what I was doing, which meant a lot to me. At the end of the day, I overstand the behavior better than anybody of why many of my homies do what they do and that is why I feel the greatest responsibility more than anybody to challenge them. We find ourselves passing on to our children, this death-style that was once accepted. We cannot continue pass this cycle of behavior on to our children, of death and destruction. Yes, I know that they have become immune to it and more importantly, adopted a self-defeating mentality however, I am dedicated to changing that culture by any means necessary.

I am always asked what type of impact I am having because in my neighborhood, people often seek some *miraculous* type of change overnight. I easily respond by saying, "I make an impact by being a

173

living and walking testament to change that people can identify with, talk to and learn firsthand from. They see that my life used to be a case study for Black failure, but today it is a case study for Black success as a result of changing my thought process, which impacted me to change my daily activity."

While I was driving through my neighborhood, a young man flagged me down. When I stopped he asked me if I could take him to the hospital and I said yes. When he got in my truck, I asked him what was wrong and he responded by saying, "I want to kill myself because I have nothing to live for!" Immediately my mind began to race as I was trying to figure out what I should do. My initial thoughts were just to drive him to the hospital, but I realized that he wasn't going to receive the type of help he needed from a hospital. So, instead of taking him to the hospital, I allowed him to pour his heart out to me about how his grandfather was dying of cancer, how he was tired of selling dope and how he want to be a productive father to his children. I listened intensely and conveyed to him that I too had traveled down the road of wanting to kill myself. I drove him to a local restaurant, treated him to lunch and we talked some more. Then we went up to my store which was under renovation. We hung out together about four hours and during our time together he began to feel better about himself and his circumstances. He eventually went home, but before he left he thanked me for being there for him. God uses us all differently do his work, we just have to be prepared when He calls upon us!

With the same intensity that pressure busts pipes, oppression drives muthafuckas to insanity! As long people are surviving in oppressive conditions while internalizing their oppression, they will continue to roam their community as socially damaged human beings committing social suicide.

I could hold my annual *Restoring the Neighbor back to the 'Hood School Supply Family Fun Day* anywhere in the City of Detroit, but I do it every year in the heart of my neighborhood Zone 8, right at my mother's house. Two years ago I decided to close off the streets and we expanded the event into a neighborhood block party. People of all ages were amazed when they saw the street blocked off and saw the city bus and police turn around and have to take another route. It was the first time in any of our lives young or old, that we were able to witness a

174

major street in our neighborhood closed off, unless it was because someone had been murdered or a house set ablaze. Many of my homies who are still heavy in the street game stopped doing what they would normally do for that day, *slanging* and *banging* and came out with their children and enjoyed the festivities. Most people wouldn't think this was a big thing for my homies to attend such an event, but the harsh reality is that guys from the *block* don't stop *slanging* and *banging* for nothing. That is their livelihood! Most of these guys ain't spending any time with their children, but on this day, they stopped what they were doing and spent quality time with their children and everybody else in the neighborhood. Also, it is a chance for my big homie Ronnie Mac, who has been using drugs for over 20 years, to have an opportunity to contribute something positive to the neighborhood and not be judged, which gives him hope and strength to fight to get that monkey off his back. During that event and others, he rides with me shot-gun as my trusted assistant, helping me pull everything together. Yes, he is a drug addict, but he doesn't allow his addiction to interfere with our business and he takes pride in the fact that I treat him as a human being.

It was a proud day, not only for the people in Zone 8, but for the entire City of Detroit. That year we added a new sponsor, a CVS from the neighborhood. Unfortunately, we didn't have enough backpacks for every household to leave with so, the District Manager Dave guaranteed me that we wouldn't have that problem the following year.

When the following year arrived, I was a man on a mission to provide 500 backpacks plus school supplies, entertainment and food to local families. I was able to bring Bank of America on as a sponsor along with CVS and City Councilman Ken Cockrel, Jr's office. The District Manager Dave from CVS was a man of his word and came through with over 150 backpacks. I enlisted my comrad Tawana "Honeycomb" Petty, to coordinate the event for me and we successfully reached our goal! When we passed out the 500 plus backpacks and school supplies, you could see the hope in the eyes of the parents and their children. For me, it is about providing families with support. We were able to relieve them from the added pressure of purchasing backpacks and some of their children's school supplies which allowed them to take the extra money and spend it on something else. It also demonstrated that someone cared for them who was not afraid to break bread with them in their neighborhood. Change starts fundamentally, when you connect to the

175

core of what you are trying to change. You have to go beyond the *surface* to get to the *root*.

As a result of my commitment and dedication, I was selected along with 20 other people around the state of Michigan who were making a difference, to receive the "Silent Heroes Award". Bankole Thompson, the Senior Editor of the Michigan Chronicle suggested me for the award and ultimately became one of my biggest supporters by writing numerous articles about me in the Michigan Chronicle. He also offered me an opportunity to contribute to his new book by interviewing me for it. It was titled, "Obama and Black Loyalty" and I was the only person from the state of Michigan to make the book out of the hundreds of interviews he conducted. I was appreciative of his support and grateful, because those on the ground doing work hardly ever get recognized. I would also receive Lakeshore Economic Coalition's "Leaders, Legends & Luminaries Award" and Bank of America's "Local Hero Award". I was in awe as I reflected upon my life and how I went from a villain to a "Leader, Local and Silent Hero. " I rationalized that as long as I rejected God's plans for me nothing ever worked for me, but once I accepted his plan for my life, things began to work in my favor. He transformed me from an underdeveloped human being (uneducated thug) to a college graduate, author and speaker. He took me from a community destroyer to a dedicated father and community activist/organizer committed to restoring the neighbor back to the 'hood. Through the grace of God, I became a champion of the people and a testament of what it meant to submit to his will. I am neither a Christian nor a Muslim, but I do believe in God. I am not a religious man, but I am spiritual man. I don't prescribe to any organized religion, but I do practice spirituality in everything I do. I don't believe I have to attend church or a temple to have a relationship with God, but I do believe my commitment to improving the quality of life affords me a strong relationship with God everywhere I find myself. Through my service to God, my mission is more clearly identified through the "Restoring the Neighbor back to the "Hood Pledge", which I co-wrote from the Black Panther pledge:

"I pledge allegiance to do my part in restoring the neighbor back to the hood. I pledge to develop myself, my family & my household to the greatest extent possible by being a shining example of a husband, father, son, brotha, wife, mother, daughter & sister in my neighborhood. I will

learn all that I can in order to give my best to improve the quality of my neighborhood. I will work diligently to honor my family in my neighborhood with good deeds & treat my neighbors as my extended family. I will keep myself mentally sound, spiritually grounded & physically fit; building a strong body, mind & spirit that will exemplify positivity & productivity in my neighborhood. I will unselfishly share my time, knowledge, resources & wisdom with my neighbors (young & old) in order to build & maintain a healthy neighborhood. I will do my part to keep my neighborhood clean & safe. I will discipline myself to direct my energies thoughtfully & constructively to maintain peace, harmony & love in my neighborhood. I will train myself to never hurt or allow anyone to harm someone in my neighborhood for an unjust cause or through negative behaviors of stealing, gun violence, verbal abuse, police brutality, selling drugs, rape or any other social ills that work to destroy my neighborhood. This is my pledge to do my part by being a caring neighbor in my neighborhood by working to keep my neighborhood a peace zone instead of a warzone."

Many of my homies and the people in my neighborhood respect the work that I do in restoring the neighbor back to the 'hood through the annual school supply drive and having my bookstore in the neighborhood. Many of the little homies come in and seek advice and many of the older people just come in to get a peace of mind. They respect the fact that I don't deal with them from the perspective of a label such as "at-risk" youth or "troubled" youth, because I believe our youth are at-risk because they are surviving in "at-risk communities" and are troubled because they are surviving in "troubled communities". Our youth have become a scapegoat for the real problems that are occurring in our community. They see through my service, that I am committed and as a result I am rewarded with their support. All the recognition I receive is because of the support and love I have received from my neighborhood Zone 8.

Because of the recognition I had been receiving based upon the work I was doing in my neighborhood and throughout the City of Detroit, I was asked by some community people to help organize a very important event called "Heal Detroit" with some up and coming Detroit community activist/organizers such as Robert Lewis Robinson, Keisha Smith and a few others. It was a march from the Eastside to the Westside of Detroit where we met up in the middle at a local park in order to

177

signify unity between both sides of the City. The event was a huge success and I delivered one of my most powerful speeches. You can youtube and watch the speech, but here is what I said:

Heal Detroit speech:
From Predators to Protectors

Detroit how do y'all feel? I feel great! But one thing I want to point out is this is not an end, but a means to an end, this is a process. And the process has to begin within ourselves. We have to stop being predators. We have to stop being predators in our community, preying on ourselves! When you're smoking weed in front of your kinds, you're preying on your kids. When you're beating on your wife, you're preying on your wife. When you're preying on the corner, doing your thing, you're preying on the grandmas and granddaddies that are afraid to walk by you. When the police come and do what they do, they're predators. We have to move from predators to protectors, protecting our community, protecting those that we say we love. If you love yourself, then you would never put yourself in harm's way. We have to stop calling our neighborhoods a 'hood, because all I know in a 'hood is drug dealers, crack sellers, gangsters and thugs. But in the neighborhood I know fathers, I know mothers; I know daughters, sons and working people. That is what we want, that is what we have to get back to! That is on us! That's not on no white man, that's on us! We need to hold ourselves accountable. You know, we're in a historical time, where we have a Black man as president, but the young men in our community is still looking up to drug dealers. They ain't looking up to Barack Obama, they looking at the drug dealers on the corners. Why?! Because that is tangible to them, and in the same process we are failing them every day. I was failed, and I ended up in prison. In prison I met my father. I went to prison and met my father! My father rehabilitated me, not prison! If left it up to prison I'd still be a thug, I'd still be a criminal. As my sista talked about in her poem "Self Hatred", that's what many of us are victimized by, self hatred. I hated myself, and by hating myself that allowed me to commit the crimes that I did, and had I not transformed and redeemed myself, I still would be committing crimes by being a predator in our community. There were a whole lot of people out here, and some of them had to leave for good reasons, but we have to be mindful that some of them came for exploitative reasons. You know, you don't see them when you need to see

178

them. Why do you only see them when it benefits them? They are predators as well preying on us using us for their own selfish purposes. And also I want to point out, too: every life is valuable in our community, not just one life! If my son dies, that shouldn't just make me want to get involved. If her son dies, his life is just as valuable as my son or any our sons, and not only should we be doing something about it, but more importantly we need to be more pro-active in our communities because by doing so there is a lot of lives that could be saved. By being reactive we are sending the wrong message, that none of us are valuable. Again we have to hold ourselves accountable. I'm mad! I'm mad because we don't see the hurt in our mother's eyes. We've got too many fathers in prison. We've got too many fathers missing in action. There's nothing wrong with being ignorant. Ignorance only means that you don't know. But there's something wrong if you want to remain ignorant. We have people that sacrificed for us to be where we are today. Love healed me, and we cannot heal Detroit until we heal ourselves. Many of us have anger and hurt in us for great reasons, but until you heal yourself, you cannot look at that person and say that's my brother, that's my sister. We cannot have peace in the neighborhoods until you have peace in your heart, peace in your mind. It starts with you. It starts with us in our neighborhood. I just walked yesterday at Mack and Beewicke, and we all know what's on Mack and Beewicke, and we brought something positive to Mack and Beewicke. And I saw the little kids eyes, and I know those kids are always going to remember that day. Somebody marched for them. No media was there, we weren't looking for any media. If you're looking for media you're at the wrong place. That's our problem. We need to start telling our stories. When I was publishing my book I didn't send my manuscript to no publishing companies, because I know no publishing company is going to promote me the way I can because it's my hurt and my pain. Which is your hurt and your pain, that's why I called it The Window 2 My Soul, because it's nothing but your soul as well. And anybody that knows Yusef knows I've been doing this a long time. This is my brotha here [Seven the General], I'm one of the guys that taught him, in gladiator school. I gave him a book, same thing my father did for me. That's what we need to start passing some knowledge! I'm just going to leave you with this. It wasn't the thought of going to prison that changed me from being a Zone 8 thug. It wasn't the thought of being killed or dying that changed me from being a Zone 8 thug. It was new information! New information that changed me! That made me see the world different, and demanded me to act different!

179

Detroit:
The Good, The Bad & The Ugly

Chapter 12

I was the product of a teenage love affair. I was raised by my mother in the concrete urban jungles of amerikkka and co-parented by the mean streets of Detroit. By the age of 15, I would be expelled from every public school I attended and in and out of the youth homes for numerous assaults, robbery and ultimately attempted murder. At the age of 19, I was sent to prison for a crime I did not commit. In prison I met my father, who rehabilitated me. Prison did not rehabilitate me!

I am *raw*, *real* and *rough* around the edges, because I am the living pain of having an alcoholic mama. I am the living hurt of being abandoned by my father. I am a result of the rawness which comes from being co-parented by the streets and imprisoned by the social ills that continue to be recycled from generation to generation. I am considered a threat, because I remind you of Bunchy Carter, John Huggins, George Jackson, Jonathan Jackson, Huey P. Newton, Fred Hampton, Mark Clark and others who were assassinated for being REVOLUTIONARIES! I am young, Black, gifted, knowledgeable, strong and committed to making a difference by being a walking testimony of *hope*, *redemption* and *transformation*. I became high in demand because I speak honestly of the social ills of Detroit and urban amerikkka while educating people regarding youth violence not only in Detroit, but across the country further reinforcing the need to become a solution oriented society.

I received a call from the Detroit NAACP asking me to attend their second meeting centered on the recent violence in Detroit. There had been a weekend shooting spree, where numerous people had been shot and killed and the NAACP wanted to get a grip on what was going on. My name was banging so hard in the streets because of the work I was doing, that people who attended the first meeting specifically requested that I be in attendance at the follow-up meeting.

When I arrived there, I noticed some faces that I had never seen before. One in particular was Deputy Chief of Police, Ralph Godbee. When it was my turn to speak, I reported exactly what the streets were

180

saying which was, "shit is a fucking war zone out here. Ain't no resources for niggas to take them from desperation to hope." I told them that in the streets, their whole thought process was centered on desperation and that their behavior was an act of desperation. I went on to say, "We have to the bridge the fucking gap between hope and desperation in order to have peace zones instead of warzones." What I said to them was like a volcano and it changed the whole context of the conversation. I know what I said was raw, but I believe it is necessary to be raw in some cases in order to educate people on what is really happening on the street level.

After the meeting, I walked out with Deputy Chief Godbee and we talked briefly. We instantly connected as brothers. We exchanged phone numbers, embraced and told each other that we loved each other. It was a powerful moment; a former Zone 8 thug and the Deputy Chief of Police embracing in the streets of Detroit for the betterment of saving lives. That was a sight to see with the Detroit Police's long history of police brutality, which reached its high mark under the notorious police squad "STRESS" which was beating and killing Black folks left and right in the early 70s. They were disbanded under the leadership of Mayor, Coleman Young after he was elected in 1974. Larry Nevers, who was once a member of the infamous police hit squad "STRESS" and his partner Walter Budzyn in November of 1992, beat Malice Green to death. They both were eventually convicted of Involuntary Manslaughter, but both of their cases were eventually overturned in the appeals court. Their cases being over turned reminded me of Supreme Court Justice Taney's assertion in the infamous Dred Scott case in 1857, which affirmed that **NO BLACK MAN HAD ANY RIGHTS THAT A WHITE MAN WAS BOUND TO RESPECT.**

The NAACP was able to pull out all the big guns for the event, from the Mayor, Detroit Police, Wayne County Sheriffs, FBI, Michigan State Police, D.A.'s office, Dr. Carl S. Taylor, local foundations, many other big named folks and all the major media outlets. Yes, I was among the elite. As we were waiting for the event to start, Dr. Taylor and I started talking in order to catch up since the last time we saw each other. I was scheduled to speak about the community so, I patiently awaited my turn while listening to all the other speakers and gathering my thoughts. I wasn't sure what I was going to say, because I never write anything down before I speak. I let the atmosphere, subject matter and the people dictate for me what I need to say. The only thing I concentrate on is speaking from my heart and with passion.

So, when it was my time to speak I described the climate of the streets as hopelessness and helplessness which was producing the underdeveloped behavior we were witnessing. Then I went on to say that "I would be doing myself and my community a disservice if I did not mention that when I met the Mayor, I gave him one of my books and he looked at me and told me that he didn't have time to read it and gave it back to me. Many people here have the same mentality of treating people who are alive, like they are dead!" There were people in the audience who started shouting "right on" after I spoke. What I said changed the complexity of the conversation. That day, I won the respect of a lot of people, but also created some enemies. Mayor Dave Bing walked right pass me and didn't even acknowledge me. What I said wasn't meant to throw him under the bus, but to expose the *ugly truth* of how certain elected officials, pastors and well off folks treat people in the neighborhoods as *peasants*. If Mayor Dave Bing would have come up to me after the event and said, "However I supposedly wronged you, I would like to fix it right now", I would have accepted that.

Once I said what I said about the Mayor, people said he had a look of a state of shock. I couldn't see him, because he was sitting on the other side of the podium. When I got up to walk off the stage, one of the Mayor's staff members who I knew ran up to me and shouted, "Yusef why did you do that?" She was standing with an older guy who I also knew, who was a huge Mayor Dave Bing supporter and he looked at me with contempt in his eyes. I dismissed her with, "what I said was the truth!" Afterwards, I was approached by the Deputy Mayor Saul Green and he pulled me to the side and kicked it with me. He let me know that despite what happened he supported me.

If you are not willing to rock the boat, go against the grain, be the thumb amongst fingers, say what is unpopular or politically incorrect and challenge people to be better human beings, then you are not ready to be an *agent of change* and you are doing a disservice to humanity. The days of *going along to get along* are long over. As I previously stated, I have been invited to a lot of meetings and events and often, they would expect for me to be the fly on the wall. However, once I opened up my mouth to speak, I became an elephant in the room. I am a force from the streets and prison and I demand to be respected.

President Obama sent a team of folks from the Department of Justice to meet with six different cities to strategize in order to come up with a plan of action to deal the violence in those cities. Detroit was one of the cities selected. One morning I was driving and received a phone call from Dr. Taylor informing me of the meeting and that I had been requested by Deputy Mayor Saul Green to be there. I shot over to where the meeting was held and shared as much as I could from my life experience. I concluded by saying, "If we are not addressing the wretched social conditions that are murdering the spirits of human beings every day, then we are only dealing with the surface of the problem. We have to dig deep and deal with the root of the problem, which is producing hopeless human beings. As long as there is no hope, there will be no peace. We bring hope, peace and love back through restoring the neighbor back to the hood!" I was well received by the folks from the Department of Justice and they all purchased a copy of my book.

When you look at the overall climate of Detroit, it is a city of great potential and promise. It has a rich history and beautiful people, but unfortunately we have many politicians, pastors, business and community folks who are unqualified to lead. Detroit, we need leadership that believe in the people and are willing to demonstrate their love for us through their actions. We need leadership that is willing to represent that we are all one, because what impacts one, impacts us all. We need leadership that will not hesitate to make the sacrifices to lead us back into glory. We need bold and honest leadership that is rooted in serving the people. Mayor Bing once promised if he was elected as the Mayor of this great city, that he would only take $1 dollar per year and donate the rest of his salary to the Detroit Police Department. It was recently reported that in July, 2011 he began collecting a salary of $158,558. That is dishonest politics or as a matter of fact, his actions continue to have Detroit bathing in "politricks."

This past summer Mayor Bing endorsed a non-profit campaign which raised $10 million for their "I'm A Believer Campaign" and they actually spent all $10 million on advertisement! There were numerous billboards throughout Detroit with different people on them and the words, "I am a Believer". I support the concept of the campaign, but where they fucked things up for me was using people who didn't live in Detroit besides rapper "Trick-Trick" and now Chief of Police Ralph Godbee and maybe one or two other people. It further angered me when I thought about what $10 million could have done for the citizens of Detroit, if it were spent the right way. The fact that they were able to raise that type of funding for something like advertising, when there are thousands of abandoned homes and homeless citizens wondering the streets of Detroit, did not sit well with me.

Detroiters couldn't identify with the people in the billboards. They did not give them a sense of pride about the city that they live in. As a native Detroiter, a believer in Detroit is the young person who has navigated through gang wars, drug wars and from broken homes to graduate from high school and earn a full scholarship to college. A believer in Detroit is the father that can't catch a break, but keeps getting up every morning giving his best while fighting against incredible odds. A believer in Detroit is the mother who is raising four children by herself, working and going to school, but not letting her challenges knock her down. She keeps pushing forward for herself and her children. A believer in Detroit is the grandfather and grandmother who have watched Detroit change over the last 40 years for the worse, but refuse to leave, because they want to stick around to see her rebirth. These are real life Detroiters that demonstrate every day that they are believers in Detroit. But you have to have your finger on the pulse of the people to know this and more importantly, to realize that real change comes from the bottom and not from the top.

Mayor Dave Bing's decision to "downsize" the City of Detroit is a direct result of him being out of touch with the city he was elected to be the Mayor of. The sad reality is that he was elected as Mayor based on the mere notion that he was going to brings jobs to Detroit, a city that is in desperate need of jobs. Since being elected Mayor, he has bullied the unions, cut jobs and cut the city's bus routes. His decision to cut the bus routes demonstrated his lack of interconnection with the majority of people of Detroit and an act of desperation from a Mayor who is desperately trying to prove himself at the expense of the people of Detroit. Everybody and their mama knows that over 50% of Detroiters depend heavily on the bus system to get back and forth through Detroit and other neighboring cities. Instead of donating a portion of his salary to hire more police, which hasn't had an impact on reducing crime, that money could have been used to keep those bus routes running which served the needs of Detroiters going to work, school and other places. If he actually stayed in Detroit before he decided to run for Mayor and actually interacted with the people in a meaningful way, he would have known that.

Mayor Dave Bing supports a vision for Detroit that does not include the people who are at the bottom. This has been clearly evident in the unconditional support he is receiving from corporate and private institutions. Reported in the Detroit News on the front page: "The Kresge Foundation confirmed Wednesday it is paying the undisclosed salary for Toni Griffin... she is expected to begin this month under an unusual arrangement." Toni Griffin was a big name urban developer who was brought in from out of state to help in the downsizing of Detroit. Mayor Bing is in bed with these private and corporate institutions to serve their interests and not the interests of the people who elected him. When he announced the whole "downsizing" agenda, he never clearly articulated what that means to Detroiters; because it is obvious he doesn't know himself. Even during one of his *State of the City Addresses,* he failed to clarify what "downsizing" Detroit actually means. Is destroying abandoned buildings and houses "downsizing" Detroit? That is the new language he used once he realized the people didn't care for his whole downsizing idea. When the decision to "downsize" Detroit was announced by Mayor Bing, it created fear and panic among Detroiters. Detroiters are already surviving in chaotic conditions so what sense does it make for the supposed leader of Detroit to present an idea that would create more chaos? I strongly believe Detroiters have no problem with **TOUGH DECISIONS**, but we do have problems with decisions that don't have our best interest at heart. The decision to "downsize" Detroit didn't include a conversation with native Detroiters. Again, it only included private and corporate institutions and those who are privileged. They have a vision of Detroit that they feel has to be imposed upon Detroiters. When he finally brought Detroiters to the table, it wasn't to hear our voices, but to hear a plan that was *sailing us down the river*.

There are neighborhoods in Detroit that resemble war torn countries and people in those neighborhoods have been surviving in Third World conditions over the last 50 years. The actions of Mayor Bing and the former Emergency Financial Manager Robert Bobb are the result of two individuals who have been manipulated by private and corporate foundations and institutions willingly. Robert Bobb was receiving a salary from private foundations that promoted privatization, while he oversaw the dismantling of DPS. Mayor Bing's decision to "downsize" Detroit and former Emergency Financial Manager Robert Bobb's decision to close over 40 schools in Detroit were both heavily influenced by private Foundations.

Many of these private Foundations have helped to contribute to the decay of many Detroit neighborhoods and schools, by openly selecting certain schools and neighborhoods in Detroit to invest money in. Through their initiatives, they have truly fooled the people by supposedly investing money in certain schools and neighborhoods, while openly denying support to other schools and neighborhoods that are deteriorating. The truth of the matter is that Detroit Public Schools and Detroit as a whole, has suffered from the games many of these private Foundations, as well as private corporations have played with the lives of Detroiters and particularly the lives of our children.

The actions of Mayor Bing and Bobb are not what is most disturbing to me. I am most disturbed by the lack of outcry by so-called religious, political and community leaders regarding the actions of these two individuals. It's obvious that many of the so-called religious, political and community leaders are in bed with Bing and Bobb, hence the reason for the inaction. Almost two years ago here in Detroit, many of the well known religious leaders spoke out loudly and proudly against the strip clubs. However, these same religious leaders have remained silent on the issues of "downsizing" Detroit and the dismantling of DPS through the closing of over 60 schools in Detroit under Robert Bobb. When you drive through many of Detroit neighborhoods and you see closed schools, it sends a message to the people, particularly the children, that their education doesn't matter and it kills their spirit.

186

Many Detroiters have decided to pick themselves up and begin to organize through the community campaigns of restoring the neighbor back to the hood, peace zones for life, food justice, community gardens and digital justice and through music and arts in order to redefine, rebuild, reeducate and re-spirit Detroit from the bottom up. We have all realized that we have to stand together, organize around one heartbeat and speak with one voice as a unified Detroit through community outreach programs which are impacting, educating and empowering the people. It is an ongoing struggle for us all to put our ideological and petty differences aside and come together for the betterment of the people of Detroit, because the world is watching us and anticipating our return to glory.

With my past clearly behind me, I was focused on my future by continuing to put my best foot forward as a community organizer and activist. I was nominated for Steve Harvey's "Hoodie Award for Best Community Leader" and I was honored. I began to promote my nomination and received some criticism for my promotion from a local activist. Actually, I respected his criticism and welcomed it, but I had strong issues with how it was addressed to me, because he deemed my actions as "selfish promotion". I strongly believe constructive criticism is a prerequisite to self development, but don't be critical of me if you don't have my best interest at heart!

My first nomination for Steve Harvey's "Hoodie Award for Best Community Leader" was a shot in the dark in 2010, but in 2011, I was nominated again. Being nominated again, spoke to the actual work that I was doing and the impact it was having on people locally and nationally. There are folks that do the work for "show" and to get recognition, then there are folks who do the work for "sho" and get no recognition. The recognition I was receiving was because of the people. I again enlisted the help of my comrad Honeycomb, who ultimately acted as my Campaign Manager by promoting me continuously and setting up a makeshift Campaign Headquarters with the permission and support of Alicia Marion and John George at their Motor City Java House in Detroit. I hit the streets from 7AM to 6PM when the votes were tallied up, rallying up further support. With Honeycomb help, the help of people locally and nationally and my work in the streets, I was announced as the top vote getter the morning of the nomination and throughout Steve Harvey's radio program. I was going back and forth from between first and fifth place and right before he went off the air, I was back in the number one spot. I was driving on the express way when Steve Harvey said the number one vote getter so far is Yusef Shakur! I almost got into a car accident, because I was so excited. About two weeks passed before they announced the top four vote getters for round one. The top four vote getters would be carried over to the second round. I texted someone I knew who worked at the radio station and she mentioned that I had just missed the top four by a few votes. I was disappointed, but I appreciated the thousands of votes I was able to receive not only in Detroit, but nationally and internationally in order to come in at number five.

Things were looking up for me, especially when a long time friend of Grace Lee Boggs contacted me about coming to Muskegon Heights, Michigan and speaking and doing a book signing. They paid for travel, housing and for speaking. Dr. Jackson is a long time activist in his own right who helped to build the first Afrikan Amerikkkan museum in Muskegon Heights a few years ago. He is also one of the first Black doctors in Muskegon Heights. Going back there and speaking afforded me an opportunity to see an elder Black woman named Ms. Betty who used to come into the prisons in Muskegon and invest her time and energy into the Black prisoners for the purpose of us changing our lives. She was extremely proud once she found out that I had been one of her students and saw the fruit of her labor. They enjoyed my presentation so much that they brought me back again and a young sister name Naeink brought me back another time to keynote their annual "Black Unity Rally". Muskegon Heights, Michigan treated me as a long lost son.

One day I was sitting at home and I received a phone call from an elder lady from Mt. Pleasant, Michigan who read about me from an article written up on me in the Detroit News. Her name was Marsha and she was a retired white teacher for alternative education. She was shocked that I answered my phone and thought she was going to talk to someone else. I take pride in building a personal relationship with my supporters and it demonstrates that I am on the same level as them. She conveyed to me that she was moved by the article that was written about me and was inspired to read my book. After reading my book, she felt compelled to call me. I told her I was honored that she called and that she made my day. Before she got off the phone, she also expressed to me that she wanted to bring me to Mt. Pleasant, Michigan to speak, because as she stated, "it is some white people in Mt. Pleasant that need to hear you." Marsha stayed true to her word and brought me to Mt. Pleasant, Michigan to do a book signing and to speak to Oasis Alternative High School. Both events went very well. A student from the alternative high school wrote me a letter after I spoke at the school for a second time:

Well once again I just want to say thank you. It was great to see you again, I'm thankful that you could hear me out and bother to come to Oasis that's real and I respect that so much. Your words mean a lot to me and every time I've listened to you speak they've made an impact in my life and helped me come to some kind of understanding. You're very inspirational and I know you hear that all time but I mean that in the most sincere way. Listening to you takes me out of my current situation and makes my future goals seem more realistic. I can take my life and see that this is temporary and if I work I can get to where I want to go. I could go on and on but overall you helped me so much, you should know you change people's lives that's a beautiful thing. I can't find the words to describe how much these last three days meant it was perfect timing for me, I needed it. I've been told that right when you feel like giving up somehow you'll find the strength not to, your words are helping me do that right now. I have so much respect for you and I look up to you. So overall thank-you for everything.

-Hannah

As I was becoming more in demand for speaking, I had to put more of a demand in being paid for my services. Most people wanted me to come and bare my soul and depart with a pat on the back and in some cases I didn't mind doing that. However, I knew that many of these non-profits, churches and schools had budgets for speakers and I expected to be paid for my services just like anybody else. Since I wasn't with any so called, big time company or wasn't some so called, big time name, they felt they could give me some bullshit and I was supposed to accept it. I wasn't having any of that. Either they would pay me or I was good. I offered a service, a damn good service and demanded the right to be paid for my service just like the next person. However, if the person who contacted me was straight up with me about their budget, I would be open to working with them for the benefit of the youth, students or men I was being requested to speak in front of. That is what I am committed to, but I refused to allow myself to be openly exploited and used because the work I do is also my job and how I take care of my family and myself. I had to learn how to manage being a community activist as well as being a businessman. During my earlier speaking engagements, I would speak at an event and would receive a standing ovation, but forget to mention that I had a book for sell, because I felt like I was taking advantage of the people. I had to realize that promoting my book was not exploiting people and that their support of me allowed me to do more.

Being a community organizer/activist is a lonely and payless job for the most part. It will always be a catch 22 shit-uation, because people have herd mentalities and follow what the media is shoving down their throats. When I sell a book I am putting that money directly in the tank of my car. When I do get a speaking gig that money is already spent on a bill I am behind on. Then for the most part, I am doing this 99% by myself and I had to figure it out without a manual. The brand *Yusef Bunchy Shakur* embodies the community activist, which is a person who serves my community relentlessly. The businessman is how I provide for my family and myself through speaking, conducting workshops, trainings and selling my books. Then you have the father, who enjoys being with my sons and in my community. I am just a simple man with a big heart and a lot of passion, which makes me seem larger than life. Out of necessity, I force myself to promote what I do to a large audience in order to generate the necessary support to be able to sustain the work that I do. Many people confuse *Yusef the persona* with *Yusef the shy person*. Being an activist, organizer and looked upon as a leader has been the hardest thing I have ever done.

The pressure my shoulders carries eats at my soul many days. There are no days for me to take off as an activist and just be a spectator and listen and learn from others and actually depend on others. There are numerous days I just break down and cleanse my soul with tears. It is the many nameless and faceless human beings (young & old, Black & white) that I meet who feel inspired by my words and actions, who in return give me the strength to continue to push forward. One of the reasons that I relish going out of town is because it allows me to learn, listen and be a regular person. I accept who I have become and I am aware that I still have a lot of growing to do, because by no means am I a finished product. Being a leader is not an easy job, especially when you have people coming up to you saying I want to follow you. That scares the hell out of me, but I overstand it comes with the territory. I didn't choose this path, it chose me. I have embraced it with all my heart and despite

190

my many successes; I know I have made a ton of mistakes without having a road map to follow! I am committed to the bloody end, in being a souljah/leader for the people.

I have been called a self-centered person because of the way I promote myself, but those same people are not making sure that my family is provided for and have no problem in promoting themselves and their product. I am an author, educator, business owner, organizer, activist and speaker so why shouldn't I promote what I do? I will never apologize for promoting what I do, which is the services that I offer. I have fought tooth and nail to get where I am at. Nobody came to show me the process, nor was there any place for me to go and ask for the help. I had to figure things out the best way I could and I will be the first person to acknowledge that I have made numerous mistakes during the process of figuring it out. Most people fail to overstand that not only did I write my book, but I run my own publishing company, a bookstore and then some. I have no choice but to promote what I do, because if I don't, I won't be able to take of care my family. It's like telling a slave that he or she doesn't have a right to fight with whatever he or she gets their hands on to free themselves. We can't talk about creating alternative visions and then want to limit how we realize those alternative visions. But through all the politics/politricks, I remain focused with the overstanding that I am nothing but a tool being used by God to help rebuild human beings!!!

One thing I've learned is that the hardest thing to do is the right thing, because even though the end result is rewarding it is a long and difficult journey to the end. On many days when you do the right thing, you will receive little to no support. It is like running a marathon and there is no one at the finish line waiting to give you a bottle of water. It is like lifting weights and not having a spotter there to make sure the weights don't cave into your chest. It is like playing in a very important sports game and when you look out into the bleachers, there is no one in the crowd there to root you on. Again, being an activist is a lonely and unappreciative journey sometimes. You have to stay focused on why you are doing what you are doing and never lose your connection to the people, because at your lowest point somebody you don't know will tell you how much what you are doing has changed their life or is making a positive impact on them.

One day I received a phone call from a young woman requesting that I meet with her and her roommates. Upon meeting with them I learned that they were community organizers from Lutheran Volunteer Corps based here in Detroit. They had heard me speak at a community event and were impressed with my speech as well as the work that I was doing on the ground level in Detroit. As the meeting progressed, they asked me if they could name their community house after me because they are part of a national organization where all of the houses across the country are named after a famous community activist/organizer. They went on to say that I exemplified what it meant to be a grassroots organizer/activist and they wanted all the new volunteer corps that came to Detroit to embody my spirit. I was speechless, honored and humbled by the experience! It's moments like that which fuel my soul to continue to fight the good fight under daunting circumstances.

I am a firm believer that without finances we will always be circling the wagon and in a position to be oppressed, as well as exploited. A lack of finances can further devalue us as human beings, where we find ourselves stuck in a mode of underdevelopment. It is a double edged sword I find myself in. The more I continue to grow and develop; I am looked at as acting funny by family members and neighborhood folks. With activist folks, the more I explore corporate ways to promote myself, the more I am looked at as being self-centered. By Black Nationalist folks, the more I look to expand by working with white people, the more I am looked at as selling out. By my street people, the more I am challenging them to better themselves, the more I am looked at as an outsider. I am rejected by the corporate people because I choose not to play their game. *So it's like, damn if I do, damn if I don't!* What I do is both personal and professional so, it is a fine line that I walk and finding the balance is not easy.

One thing I do overstand is that everybody may not have the time to get involved in organizing a project or an event that will make a difference in our community, but everybody has the time to support those who are doing that type of work. There is no excuse, everybody has a role to play no matter how big or small it may be. That is how we restore the neighbor back to the 'hood, by everybody doing their part.

Having my books used in different universities such as Michigan, Michigan State, Central Michigan, Wayne State and Wayne

192

County Community afforded me the great opportunity to speak in front of classes where the students could ask me questions after reading my book. After speaking at the University of Michigan I received a phone call from an older white woman who wanted to meet with me so, I invited her to my bookstore. When she arrived, she began by telling me that her daughter was a student in the class I spoke in and her daughter loved my book, but was more impressed with my presentation. So, she suggested that her mother do a story on me, because she is a writer at the Detroit News. Her mother felt compelled by her daughter's request and did the story. It would be the first time my story would be written about in any of the major newspapers here in Detroit. When I first wrote my book, I never sent out a press release about it, because at that time I never knew anything about a press release and to this date, I still haven't sent one out. My work and story have been so strong that I have been featured in writes up, on TV and radio locally and across the country. This past summer BBC World Service contacted me about an interview and sent a reporter here to Detroit. They are the world's largest international broadcaster. I was also recently asked to write a blog for the Huffington Post. Below you will find a letter I received from someone who heard my BBC interview:

Dear Mr Shakur,

I've been having a hard time recently. Sometimes at night I can't sleep........ Last night I reached for the radio and there was your voice, talking about Detroit. I have seen photographs of the devastation in some of the Detroit neighborhoods .... How strange it was, lying in bed in the middle of the night in England, to hear your moving and inspiring story. Straight away I wished I could visit Detroit and join you in your work. I wonder what the future holds for our strange and unfair Western capitalist system. Somebody said that the decline of an Empire is always preceded by a vast increase in "private wealth and public squalor". That is happening today in America and the UK too. In London we have the "super-rich", buying houses for $100 million and we have the super-poor too. You may have heard about our riots recently. I don't think the wealthy have any idea how hard life is for the unemployed and the working poor. Our new "coalition" government is busy cutting back on public services and destroying our Welfare State. The cuts are infiltrating all corners of life. The full effect will not be felt until months and years ahead and the worst is yet to come. I heard that in Detroit

*some people are planting gardens and growing food for the Community.
And you opened a bookstore to cultivate and open the mind ....I work in
education (16-19 year olds) and I'm continually struck by how little the
kids know. Their worlds are very small. They listen to their iphones and
have their hair done. They have no idea what is going on. Thank you
very much for making this programme with the BBC World Service.
People all over the world will have heard your voice by now ..... How
inspiring that people like you exist in the world, helping others and
encouraging the young to stretch themselves, to rise up within
themselves, to aspire ......I feel inspired by your example. I wish you and
all your co-workers continued success with your projects*

> *May you be happy.*
> *May you be peaceful.*
> *May you be free from suffering.*
> *May you be at ease.*
> *Best wishes from Isabelle in England.*

For the most part, when I speak at colleges it is in front of 90%
white students. Many of them have questions about Detroit and some of
them ask how a white person can help Detroit. I don't hesitate by saying,
"first not by coming with a white missionary mentality thinking you are
here to save Detroit. You have to become a part of the fabric of Detroit
because oppression, exploitation, pain and hurt transcend skin color. Not
being from poverty doesn't mean you can't help, but having a genuine
heart and a willingness to meet people where they are qualifies you to
help!" In the movie Malcolm X, there is a scene where a young white
lady asks Malcolm how she can help and Malcolm responds by saying
that she can't help. I believe there is something white people can do,
which is to go back to their homes, churches, schools and communities
and fight racism/white supremacy. That is the best thing any white
person can do if they want to help people of color. Racism and white
supremacy is the greatest threat to humanity and we all have an
obligation to fight against it.

I, like Malcolm X once learned it is not the color of a person's
skin that can tell you who they are, but it is through their actions. I do
believe there are millions of white people who are still racist than a
muthafucker, but I also believe there are some good white people who
want to make a difference. Some that I know personally who are doing

194

just that such as Andrew, Mrs. Gallagher, Marsha, Kerry, Richard, Shea, Linda, Professor Kinney at CMU, Karen, Pastor Bill and numerous others that I have met who have supported me and other people of color, unconditionally. Long time Detroit activist Marian Kramer recently expressed to me that I shouldn't just see myself as a leader for Black people, but white people as well and her words made all the sense in the world to me. When I was recently back up in Mt. Pleasant, Michigan speaking to white high school students and college students, many of them came up to me after I bared my soul to them. This was a reflection of their souls as well as all the pain and hurt they have been carrying around from been fucked over and abused. I had the great honor to speak at Central Michigan University (CMU) in front of close to 300 students, with majority of them being white. When I was done speaking, a young Black student came up to me and said, "You know you just scared the hell of these people" and we laughed. Then a young white student came up to me and said after hearing me speak it re-enforced that he had made the right decision of not wanting to be racist like the rest of his family.

I have been educated by many of the white students that I speak to who relate to my story of being a child of an alcoholic mother and not having a father in my life. They have helped me to recognize that it is not a Black problem, but it is a human problem and as a result of experiencing these social ills we have all been hurt and scarred. We have an obligation as human beings to help in the healing of all human beings from the pain and hurt that is plaguing our lives and stagnating our growth and development as human beings.

When you look at a City like Detroit which is 85% Black, it is basically a segregated city in the north. People fail to overstand that the lack of human relations are not developed as a result of the segregation in this city and state. I have never had any white people live in my neighborhood or attend any of the schools I attended in my youth. For the most part, my only meaningful interaction with white people had been from the stand point of them controlling my life as a judge, prosecutor, police, counselor, case worker, probation officer, parole officer and prison guards which ultimately re-enforces white supremacy and Black inferiority in amerikkka. Those experiences wouldn't allow me to have a healthy outlook of myself and my community that is rooted in Black inferiority and most white people view Black people from

195

unhealthy viewpoints rooted in racism/white supremacy, which is contributing to poor human relationships between us all.

Over the last couple of years white people have been moving back into Detroit and have created pocket communities in "Mid-Town" and "Cork-Town", which are considered to be model communities. I believe there are some well-meaning white people living in those white pocket communities who want to make a difference in the City of Detroit, but they have become marginalized in those pocket white communities, because of the segregated shit-uation here in Detroit. I am not afraid of white people moving back to Detroit. We should welcome it. However, many Detroit Black residents are influenced by the *urban myth* that white people are coming back to take Detroit from us, which is fed by the many politicians that continue to sell Detroit out to the highest *white bidder*. Detroit can't be a strong city without strong neighborhoods. They can invest all the money in the world in Downtown Detroit, Mid-Town and Cork-Town, but if they continue to neglect Detroit neighborhoods, people who live in downtown, mid-town and cork-town will be nothing but a potential victim by a person who sees them as a possible opportunity to feed themselves. Reshaping Detroit has to start with reshaping the neighborhoods.

This was my issue with the recent movement "occupy Detroit", which was a spinoff of the movement in New York called "occupy Wall Street" where people protested in Time Square against the big banks. Detroit, along with cities and states across amerikkka cloned the movement for their respective locations. However, the Detroit clone did not reflect nor speak to the concerns and needs of Detroiters, which are 90% people of color and most of the "occupiers" acted as if we were supposed to be happy that white people were coming to help. *Fuck that*, Black and Brown Detroiters have been suffering for too long to go out like that. In New York it wasn't called "occupy New York", it was called "occupy Wall Street", which made all the sense in the world. Why do Detroiters need to occupy a space they already occupy? What we need is *liberation*, not *occupation*!

I went to the first general assembly here in Detroit and it was predominantly white. The meetings after that were the same. I decided to reach out to Jenny Lee whom I respected as an activist and she had a mutual respect for me so, we deiced to write a letter to the first general assembly:

To the first General Assembly of Occupy Detroit,

We are inspired by the actions of Occupy Wall Street and the opportunity it has given so many people to stand up and get involved in shaping the fate of this country. We are inspired by the protocol of consensus decision-making and inclusivity being used on Wall Street, where anyone who shows up is asked: "what can you contribute to this movement?" And they are supported to bring their best selves to the work of creating a new world. We propose that Detroit embrace that same protocol. In the spirit of bringing our best selves to this process, we offer this background knowledge, which anyone attempting to organize in Detroit must first understand before taking any action that aims to speak for Detroit.

Detroit is a Movement City. *Detroiters have been organizing resistance to corporate greed and violence for nearly a century, from the birth of the labor movement here in the 1920s to the current poor people's campaigns against utility shutoffs that kill dozens of people each year. We have organized resistance to racism, sexism, homophobia, and the criminalization of youth, to the systematic destruction of the environment in poor communities of color, to the dehumanization of people with disabilities, and so many other injustices -- as they manifest in policy, and in our everyday lives.* ***Detroit has moved beyond protest.*** *Because we have survived the most thorough disinvestment of capital that any major U.S. city has ever seen; because we have survived "white flight" and "middle class flight," state-takeovers, corruption and the dismantling of our public institutions; because the people who remained in Detroit are resilient and ingenious, Detroiters have redefined what "revolution" looks like.* ***Detroit is modeling life after capitalism.*** *In Detroit, "revolution" means "putting the neighbor back in the hood" through direct actions that restore community. It means Peace Zones for Life that help us solve conflict in our neighborhoods without the use of police, reducing opportunities for police violence. It means food justice and digital justice networks across the city supporting self-determination and community empowerment. It means youth leadership programs and paradigm-shifting education models that transform the stale debate between charter schools and public schools. It means "eviction* *reversals" that put people back in their homes and community safety networks that prevent people being snatched up by border patrol. It means artists that facilitate processes of community visioning and transformation, and organizers who approach social change as a work of art. In Detroit, the meaning of "revolution" continues to evolve and grow. **Detroit will not be "occupied."** The language of "occupation" makes sense in the context of Wall Street, but it will not inspire participation in Detroit. From the original theft of Detroit's land by French settlers from Indigenous nations, to the connotations of "occupation" for Detroit's Arab American communities, to the current gentrification of Detroit neighborhoods and its related violence -- "Occupation" is not what we need more of. Detroit's participation in the "Occupy Together" actions must grow out of Detroit's own rich soil. It cannot be transplanted from another city's context. We recognize that "Occupy Detroit" has attracted the participation of people from across the state of Michigan. This is a good thing, IF people take the time to understand the unique history and current work of Detroit's social movements. This letter aims to be a starting point in that process.*

Yusef Shakur & Jenny Lee

There were a lot of genuine white people who had migrated into Detroit through the occupy movement who wanted to make a difference, but the movement they came through wasn't rooted in the *current* shit-uation of Detroit, which prevented them from helping in a meaningful way. The occupy movement missed an opportunity to deal with the great racial divide that exists in this city and state and many of the occupiers, Black and white had no clue of what a movement was, or what it meant to be an activist. They were ignorant to the past movements and in particular to COINTELPRO. None of them realized that they had already been infiltrated by the police and those who did know, didn't care. For them, it was an opportunity to stick it to the man and be a part of the revolution. Revolution is not an act of protest. It is an organized motion of people dedicated to seizing power. There is a huge difference between REFORM and REVOLUTION!

The first 19 years of my life, my travels were restricted to my neighborhood Zone 8, precincts, youth homes, county jails and prisons. During the last three years of my life, my travels have taken me to North Carolina, Muskegon, Mt. Pleasant, Wisconsin, Alabama, Chicago (twice), Washington D.C. (twice), Oakland (twice), L.A. (twice), New Orleans, San Francisco and New York (twice). Being able to travel has been a life changing experience which has allowed me to grow as a human being and activist.

Going to Alabama to be a part of the delegation of formerly incarcerated people to discuss a national agenda to demand our human rights and civil rights, was powerful. We left Alabama as an organized body growing into a movement through the voice of "Formerly Incarcerated and Convicted Peoples Movement (FICP). We followed Alabama up with our first national convention in L.A. this pass year in November, 2011. Over 200 from across the country people attended from formerly incarcerated, convicted people, family members of those still incarcerated and supporters and we presented our national platform to them. We followed up the L.A. gathering with a gathering in New Orleans where we began to organize our infrastructure as a movement, and I was selected as the Chair of the National Literature Committee. Below you will find an excerpt from our national platform:

Formerly Incarcerated & Convicted Peoples Platform

II. We Demand Equality and Opportunity for All People

III. We Demand the Right to Vote

IV. We Demand Respect and Dignity for our Children

V. We Demand Community Development, Not Prison Profit

VI. End Immigration Detention and Deportation

VII. End Racial Profiling Inside Prison and In Our Communities

VIII. End Extortion and Slavery in Prisons

IX. End Sexual Harassment of People in Prison

X. Human Contact is a Human Right

XI. End Cruel and Unusual Punishmen

XII. We Demand Proper Medical Treatment

XIII. End the Incarceration of Children

XIV. Free Our Political Prisoners

I had the great honor of returning back to the Bay area to attend the 45th Anniversary of the Black Panther Party this year and I met rank and file members from across the country. I also got a chance to meet Bobby Seal the founding "Chairman" of the BPP with Huey P. Newton. It was great to sit and watch the brothers and sisters just congregate, laugh and share stories good and bad. I admire the comradeship that they shared with one another that was built through blood and struggle. I took my "Seize Time" book written by Bobby Seal and had all the members sign it. I was talking with a former panther and gave him my business card and he noticed that my name was Bunchy so; he immediately asked what I knew about Bunchy. I respond by saying "I named myself Bunchy in honor of Bunchy Carter, who was a member of the Black Panther Party and was murdered by the police. In Bunchy I saw who I used to be, because he was a member of a gang in California in the late 60s and ultimately went to prison as well, where he transformed his life. Also through Bunchy I saw what I could become by his coming home from prison and joining the Black Panther Party and being a leader in his community as well as making a difference. Shakur is in honor of the many east coast Black Panthers. In Afrikan tradition a name is essential to guiding a person to becoming a great human being, because every time they hear their name they are constantly reminded of what their name means." The elder brother gave me a clenched-fist salute and said, "right on young brother!"

It was a wonderful experience and on my way back to Detroit I realized that through me and other young Black/Brown/white activists across this country, that the *Black Panther Party, Brown Berets/Students for a Democratic Society lives* on. I remembered that revolutionaries don't fall out of the sky or crawl out of the ground. We are created by our conditions/circumstances. We are shaped through our studying/reading. We are developed through our work with the people. We are motivated by love. We embrace sacrifice, because that is part of the struggle. We don't hate our enemy, but we do hate oppression. We are not afraid of death, because we overstand through death brings life. We are committed to education, because it provides us with our vision. To be a revolutionary, is to be a nation builder and as a revolutionary, we must be a reflection of a new human being and a new society we wish to build with the people. To be a revolutionary is not to be a leader of the people, but to be a servant of the people because he/she overstands that the people are the leaders and we serve them out of a labor of love!

One day I received a phone call from Richard Feldman about some folks coming to Detroit from the "Annenberg Foundation" to interview some folks and he mentioned my name to them. When they arrived in Detroit, they spent a day with me up at my bookstore and we drove through my neighborhood and other parts of Detroit and they asked me numerous questions. I received a phone call a few weeks later and was told that I, along with a few others from Detroit had each been granted a $25,000 grant. I used the money to remodel the bookstore and expand it into a cyber café. My consistent and hard work had put me in a position to receive the financial support to expand the work that we were doing and because of their support, we were able to create jobs for people in the neighborhood. I am grateful and appreciative of the Annenberg Foundation for their support.

For the grand opening of the Urban Network Cyber Café I flew in my comrad Sundiata from the Bay area to be a part of our "Black August" celebration. Because of the history of Black August, I felt that it was important to celebrate it by bringing Sundiata to Detroit to share his experience as being a member of the San Quentin Six and a comrade of George Jackson. This is a part of history that I took pride in being able to provide to my neighborhood Zone 8. It was a beautiful event and Sundiata is a beautiful human being. I was also happy that his Detroit trip had allowed him to see family members he had here that he hadn't seen in a long time.

After I did the renovations to the store, many people began to look at me crazy, because they couldn't overstand why would I donate that type of money into the type of environment where I could face the high probability of being broken into. I didn't concern myself with that even though I knew it was a harsh reality. Since we have been there, some of the lil homies have stolen from me twice. The first time I found out, the lil homie brought it back to me and now he comes into the store everyday asking if there is anything he can do. Another incident that showed me that we were having a positive impact was when a white college student, who had heard me speak at the U.S. Social Forum asked if she could interview me. I was like sure and invited her to the Urban Network. When I looked out the big picture window, I noticed a car pull up and the person driving looking for the address. I knew it was her. I looked again and noticed a bunch of people in front of the store. I immediately stopped what I was doing to go see what was going on. When I got outside I noticed a young white girl crying and an older white guy with blood running down his face. Further down the street, a group of Black men had detained a Black guy and was jumping on him and yelling at him.

When she had pulled up, a drug addict had attempted to snatch her purse, but she wouldn't let go and her father came to her rescue. The drug addict, who was a Black guy, had socked him trying to get away. People coming out of the liquor store observed what had happened and ran down there to help them. They were yelling at the guy, "You can't do that over here. They came to see Yusef!" On that day, people in my neighborhood declared that crime was not accepted whether you were Black or white. Despite our racial differences from that shit-uation, we became a community of human beings. They felt so compelled from the support they received, that they stayed and conducted the interview.

I frequently receive phone calls or emails from people who want to interview me about Detroit and I ask them, "How is this interview going to help me, my neighborhood or the City of Detroit?" I don't mind doing the interviews with genuine people, but if they are interested in making a mockery out of Detroit, then I will pass.

In early 2011, my comrade Shaka and I were flown out to Plateville, Wisconsin to speak to a University for the Black Student Union's, annual Black History Program. It was an incredible experience for both of us and our first time being able to bond as brothers since his release from prison after doing 19 years. Professor Karen Gagne was instrumental in getting the Black Student Union to get us out there to speak. Besides us being the keynote speakers for "Ebony Weekend", we also spoke eight times in three days. Brittany, who was the president of the BSU made it happen as well. We did such a great job speaking and connecting with the students and the professors that this past summer they flew us there again to speak at a "Racial Inclusiveness" event where

Dr. Cornel West was the keynote speaker. After we spoke in our session, we attended the larger session where Dr. Cornel West was speaking. After he spoke, we introduced ourselves to him and he purchased both of our books. He was real cool and down to earth.

While speaking at different colleges, I am often asked by college students how they can be more supportive and I respond by saying, "by reaching out to activists/organizers/community leaders to bring them to the college campus to speak." It is essential that the relationship between students and those in the community is developed, because those of us in the community are the infantry and those on the college campus are the cavalry. Every college student bares the responsibility of using the skills they learn while there and upon graduation to make this world better. We all bare that responsibility as human beings.

Also, in February of 2011, I organized a celebration honoring my being home for ten years from prison and Chief of Police, Ralph Godbee was the keynote speaker. I can only imagine what it is like to be a Black police officer in a white dominated field, where most of the people you are arresting and sending to prison are Black. I know that it was as an exciting a day for him, as it was for me, because I believe him and certain other Black police officers are in that line of work to make a difference and not just to lock up Black men. Unfortunately it is not enough of them. Also, my comrade Honeycomb recited a poem that she wrote in my honor titled, "Yusef/Detroit:

Yusef/Detroit

We were supposed to

Turn our backs on you

Anticipate your imminent demise

Dangle you by the limbs

Of misdeeds

They wanted us to rate you inferior

Plagued by deteriorating

Neighborhoods

And a convoluted history

203

You were never supposed to

Bloom from your ashes

A lot like you

Have been discarded like debris

Deemed useless to naysayers

And convictors

Yet you keep rising

Clinging to vitality

You've refused to allow statistics

To dictate your destiny

And the media

Will channel your journey

And though some shall remain loyal

Others will mock your tribulations

You were fathered into maturity

Both your gift and your curse

Imported from adversity

You've seen better decades

Yet you thrived

During the worst of them

Your best days

Have yet to arrive

And some won't stick around

To witness your climb

Or rejoice

In your restoration

But your destination

Is inevitable

You've been on the bottom

Much longer than most

And the bridges you'll journey

Won't be easy to coast

But you'll make it

And bring warriors with you

Armed with devotion

They will defend your dignity

And honor your namesake

You are Detroit

Mr. Yusef Shakur

The road to progression

The mirror image of endurance

And you hold the key

To restoring the neighbor

Back to the hood

I was riding on cloud 9 after that event and I didn't think that I could go any higher. Then, one day I was in a neighborhood store buying something and heard a Black history commercial on a major radio station. Instead of saluting Black people from the past for Black history, they were recognizing current people and even local people. The commercial was about me and was celebrating my transformation. I had no idea that they were running the commercial and when I heard it, I cried immediately. I was just taken back by it. I praised God and thanked him for allowing others to see what he had done with me.

The good news soon turned to bad as Detroit had another weekend of mayhem this year where over 16 people were shot and many of them died. I was asked to be on the Craig Fahle show on 101.9 FM to discuss the recent violence in the city. The following day, I received a phone call from Huel Perkins who hosts a late night panel discussion on Fox 2 News titled, "Let It Rip". He requested that I come on the show and I agreed, but I was shocked, surprised and nervous. I had just committed myself to appear on national television! I called a few folks who I trusted and asked them for advice and they simply said, "don't

205

change anything about you, because being you is what got you on the show." Before we went on the air Huel Perkins conveyed to me that he had heard a lot about me from different people throughout the City of Detroit and they all had nothing but good to say. I was in awe. When it was time to do the show he had mentioned he was going to show one of my youtube speeches and I was trying to figure out which one he had pulled up. He ended up showing the clip from the speech I did at "Heal Detroit". On my way home after the show, he called me and thanked me for being on and advised me that he respected the work that I was doing and that I had a supporter in him. I was honored.

A lot people look at my success get caught up in it and only befriend me because of it. They are neglectful of the nine years of work I put into it while in prison and the 11 years of work I have done since I have been home from prison. When you add those years up, I have been actively involved in activism in prison and in my community for 20 years. Nothing has been given to me. I have earned it through tears, sweat, dedication, commitment and hard work. This past summer because of my community organizing in the City of Detroit, I made the top five final nominees out of hundreds nominees across from the state of Michigan for the "Progressive Organizer of the Year" award that was handed out by Progress Michigan at their Michigan Summit. People look at the media attention I have been able to receive via radio, television and newspaper locally and nationally, which I have never sought out. *It sought me out.* Again, I have never circulated a press release for anything that I have done. I don't have a publicist working on behalf of me, even though I need one. It has been through hard work and making a difference, that I have been afforded me an opportunity to have media outlets share my story of transformation and work with the world. I have learned many people want success, but are not willing to commit themselves to doing the work. If I never received any media attention I would be fine, because I don't do the work for that. I do the work to make a difference and attribute that to God.

When you look at Detroit you have to recognize the good, the bad and the ugly. When you do this, you will realize that there is more good, than bad and ugly. Detroit needs a *people's first* mentality. It is now or never! Many politicians, pastors, non-profits and community leaders sold us out yesterday and continue to sell us out today. We have to band together to not only protect each other, but to provide for each other, share with each other, feed each other, care for each other and more importantly love each other in these tough times. Talk is good Detroit, but we need efficient and effective action. We have to take action now, before we lose another grandmother, grandfather, mother, father, son, daughter or friend mentally, spiritually or physically. We need to continue to be proactive in rebuilding and re-spiriting Detroit. We have to change the mindset and the culture of Detroit, because if we don't, all the money in the world will not help in Detroit's rebirth. The people of Detroit need a rebirth which will fuel Detroit's rebirth.

What is peace when there is no hope? We need programs that are educating, serving and empowering human beings. We need individuals who desperately want to be leaders, to be educated. Helping your neighbor or someone in the community does not make you a community activist; it makes you a good human being, which I am of the belief that we need more good human beings than activists. Activist is nothing but a label at the end of the day, but being a good human being speaks to our connection to each other and our desire restore humanity to human beings which has greater meaning. I overstand that our communities are suffering on every level and that any person who provides an act of relief towards their suffering is embraced as a savior. That is dangerous, because now our communities become depended upon individuals who aren't qualified in the first place.

We need a movement that breeds hope, that restores the humanity to human beings, which is rooted in (tough) unconditional love, has a vision that moves us from internalizing our oppression to liberating us from all types of oppression. We can't afford to lose another life, because every life is valuable!

We need people who are not afraid to make sacrifices on every level. We need people to overstand that oppression and exploitation still exists in amerikkka, which is the root cause of our misery. We need to develop and create liberated peace zones, which will breed hope amongst the people and instill high expectations within the people to treat each other like human beings and not like animals! We need people to get off their asses and fight with everything they have! We need people to overstand that we are at war and we are fighting for our lives and for future generations not to suffer like we have. We need every human being to be joining our ranks; white, Black, Brown, any color. We need people to overstand that we have to restore the neighbor back to the 'hood, if not the hood will be the death of all of us. People survive in 'hoods through underdeveloped behavior, but people live in neighborhoods through love and care. Our greatest resource is our capacity to love and care for each other and for our neighbors, which will bridge the gap between hope and desperation.

Detroit every time I leave you, I miss you even more and my love for you grows deeper. My connection to you runs as deep as the Nile River. My vision for you is as rich as the soil of Afrika. I am dedicated to restore your honor through my service of restoring the neighbor back to the 'hood. Detroit talking is not my specialty. I do it out of necessity to educate, inform and say what others are scared to say. As you know my love, I am an action person because action speaks louder than words. Action impacts people's lives. Action inspires people. Action provides different models for people to follow. Action builds relationships. Actions demonstrate love. Detroit, I will service you with the spirit of Nat Turner, I have the experience of Malcolm X to redeem you, I have a vision for you like Marcus Garvey, courage to fight for you like Huey P. Newton, passion to protect you like Tupac Shakur, I will speak the truth for you like Fredrick Douglass, be bold for you like Bunchy Carter, I have intelligence for you like W.E.B. Dubois, a Guerrilla state of mind to ride for you like Che Guevara, I will rebuild you from the bottom up like my name is Booker T. Washington and I will be courageous for you, like George Jackson while being surround by our enemies plotting your demise. Detroit I am forever dedicated to you and I will serve you in life and in death. I love you for better or worse!!!

Yusef **B**unchy **S**hakur, is a father, author, leader, bookstore/café owner, community organizer/activist, educator and public speaker. His first book, "The Window 2 My Soul" has been taught in classes at the University of Michigan, Michigan State University, Eastern Michigan University, Central Michigan University, Wayne State University, Wayne County Community College and Merritt College in Oakland, California, as well as numerous public schools throughout the state of Michigan. He has been regarded as one of the most thought provoking and outspoken voices of his generation. Shakur's voice can often be heard in auditoriums and class rooms in major universities, public schools, churches and community events across the country. He has been featured in a multitude of television programs, newspapers and radio outlets from WJLB's "Girl, Bye!", Mason Radio on 107.5 FM, the Craig Fahle Show on 101.9 FM, the Detroit News, the Detroit Free Press, the Michigan Citizen, the Michigan Chronicle, Fox 2's "Let It Rip" and the international radio program BBC World Service. Shakur has been widely recognized for his community work with such awards as the Volunteer of the Year Award 2004, Rev. Dr. Wendell Anthony's Social Activist Award 2008, the Silent Hero Award 2009, the Leaders, Legends & Luminaries Award 2010, the Local Hero Award 2010, the Malcolm X Award 2010, the 10 Years of Freedom Award 2011 and the BME (Black Men Engagement) Award 2012. He has received a "Special Tribute" from Congressman Hansen Clarke, State Representative Fred Durhal and Senator Bert Johnson; "Testimonial Resolution's" and the "Spirit of Detroit" awards from the Detroit City Council and Wayne County Commissioners." After serving 9 years in prison, Shakur became instrumental in making significant contributions to the betterment of his community. These contributions derive from his personal commitment to "**Restore the Neighbor Back to the 'Hood.**" Remaining true to his commitment by opening up a bookstore/café in his neighborhood, also he has organized various community initiatives and events in and around the City of Detroit during the past 11 years. They include, but are not limited to, providing backpacks and school supplies to more than 1000 children over the last four years. Shakur values education and has furthered his own by earning an Associates Degree.

Thank you for your support! If you would like to let the author know how you felt about the book or if you are interested in booking him for speaking engagements or workshops, please contact him via email at: yusefshakur@yahoo.com, phone 313-459-6008 or on facebook at **Yusef Bunchy Shakur.**

To place an order go to www.yusefshakur.org or send your payment to:

Urban Guerrilla Publishing
Att: Yusef Shakur
5740 Grand River
Det, Mi, 48208

"My Soul Looks Back" is available for $14.99. Please include $ 3.95 for shipping and handling. For information about special discounts for bulk purchases please contact Urban Guerrilla Publishing Division at 313 459-6008.